African Renais

Vol 4. No.1 Quarter1 2007

Contents

The Horn of Africa:
From Crises and Wars to Peace and Stability

African Renaissance
Vol.4 No.1 Quarter 1 2007
pp5-8

The Horn of Africa:
From Crises and Wars to Peace and Stability

From the Editor/Publisher

Jideofor Adibe,PhD

In the November/December 2006 issue of the journal, we focused on African culture and philosophy and their possible relationship with the current crises of governance and development in the continent. We posed a number of crucial questions: Are the current crises of governance and development in the continent facilitated by African culture and philosophy of life? Or are they the result of lack of, or insufficient incorporation of these into the models of development and

Jideofor Adibe

governance imported into the continent from outside? Are these largely imported models of governance and development culturally and philosophically neutral?

In this edition, we focus on the Horn of Africa- (also known as Northeast Africa or the Somali Peninsula)) - a peninsula of East Africa that juts for hundreds of kilometers into the Arabian Sea, and comprising Ethiopia, Somalia, Eritrea and Djibouti. While the lead theme is on the Horn of Africa, the special focus is on the two dominant players in the region – Ethiopia and Somalia. We look at the region, the problems of conflicts, dictatorships, wars, weapon proliferation, identity, and development trajectory. We ask some key questions: What political agendas, if any, do the competing historical narratives of ethnic identities serve in the region? How has the Cold War era super power rivalry affected the political configuration in the region? And how have all these affetced the form of development thoughts, and development trajectory in the region?

Daniel Aremu argues that European construction of Ethiopian historiography has largely rested on the hypothesis that the Ethiopian state and civilization were built by immigrants from South Arabia who colonized Ethiopia in the first millennium B.C. He notes that this thesis has percolated into Ethiopian politcs in the last few decades through such notions as "indigenousness" and "alieness", in which groups like Amhara and Tigreans, said to be "the children of Arab immigrants and Africans" are viewed by some Ethiopians as "aliens", and therefore colonisers of indigenous groups like Oromo and Eritrea (before its independence).

Osman Farah and Mammo Muchie reflected on the 2006 Christmas war by Ethiopia on Somalia, noting that the two countries have had two wars since Somalia's independence, the first being in 1964, which ".started because of the Somali irredentism and claim of the Ogaden region." They argue that some Somalis see Ethiopia as "a sort of substitute of 'colonial power'", and that this perception coloured Somali's perception of the recent Ethiopian intervention in the country, with American backing.

Berhanu Gutema Balcha discusses ethnicity and federalism in Ethiopia, which have "become the major factors in organizing the political and territorial space in Ethiopia since 1991," noting that "the 'ethnic- federal' experiment of devolving public sector powers to ethnic groups goes against the centralized nation-building project of the previous regimes." He accuses the Tigrayan People's Liberation Front (TPLF), which claims to represent the Tigray province and the Tigray people, of hegemonistic tendencies, despite accounting for only six percent of Ethiopia's populations.

Mohamed Haji Mukhtar discusses the collapse of the Somali state, the various peace conferences and efforts at reconstituting the failed state and the recent Ethiopian military intervention. He argues that the fall of "Mogadishu on New Year's Eve to the allied forces of the Transitional Federal Government (TFG) and Ethiopia won't hurt the Union of Islamic Court's (UIC) jihad in Ethiopia, nor will it automatically bring stability to war- torn Somalia." He however believes that "the outcome of the Ethiopian interventions and the eventual empowerment of the TFG should be looked at by both Somalis and the international community as a potential blessing in disguise."

Abdurahman M. Abdullahi discusses the history of Somali's women's political participation over four decades, noting that that although "Somali women gained full political rights before independence in 1960, it nonetheless took 40 years for them to receive a constitutionally sanctioned quota in the National Assembly.". He posited that the "landslide victory of Somali women in the Somali Reconciliation Conference of 2000 should be understood as a product of 40 years of cumulative struggle by local and international actors."

Jesiah Selvam analyses the privatisation programme in Ethiopia, which began in the 1990s, noting that the country's "national debt is perennially at the centre of economic policy debates". Fekadu Fullas discusses the role of indigenous medicinal plants in Ethiopia's healthcare, noting that "there are anywhere between 650 and 1,000 medicinal plants in Ethiopia, comprising about 10 per cent of the entire flowering plants found in the country". He argues that the key challenge in Ethiopia is "how to streamline this resource for the benefit of not only those people who do not have access to modern medicines, but also for those who fail on conventional medications, or those, who for economic reasons opt for local products which can potentially be as effective."

Besides articles in the lead theme, we also brought together various other contributions, from Professor Ali Mazrui's **LIVING LEGEND AWARD, 2007,** acceptance speech to a tribute to music superstar James Brown's, who rested in the Lord on December 25, 2006.

African Renaissance: Book Series

African Renaissance, a multidisciplinary journal, which we launched as a bi-monthly in June 2004, has become a quarterly from this year and this issue – after 15 consecutive issues, without missing a deadline. Late last year, the journal launched some book series such that some of the articles published in the journal are updated/revised/extended in a book of
African Journal of Business and Economic Research: Book Series

AJBER: Book Series

African Journal of Business and Economic Research, a triennial, peer-reviewed academic journal, which made its debut in January last year, also launched a book series. The first in the book series **Management and Economic Development in sub-Saharan Africa: Theoretical and Applied Perspectives** will be published on March 20.
For details of the journal, including how to contribute, please contact its editor Dr John Kuada at: kuada@business.aau.dk   For sales enquiries, please contact: sales@adonis-abbey.com

African Performance Review

APR, a triennial, peer-reviewed journal of the African Theatre Association (AfTA) debuts on March 29 2007. To contribute to the journal, contact:
The Editor, (Dr Osita Okagbue)
African Performance Review
Department of Drama, Goldsmiths, University of London,
SE14 6NW United Kingdom. Tel: +44 (0)207 919-7581.
Email: AfTA@gold.ac.uk.

Review of Nigerian Affairs

RVN, a quarterly multidisciplinary journal of Nigerian politics and society debuts in on March 31 2007. The journal is a cross between an academic publication and any quality newsfeature publication. To contribute to the journal, contact:
editor@adonis-abbey.com (Dr Jideofor Adibe).
For sales enquiries, please contact: sales@adonis-abbey.com

Dr Jideofor Adibe is the Editor of *African Renaissance*, and Publisher, Adonis & Abbey Publishers Ltd, London.

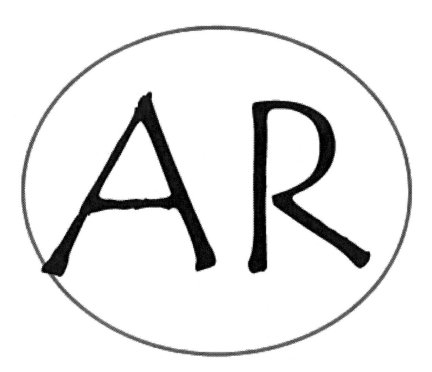

To contribute to
African Renaissance
please contact:
editor@adonis-abbey.com

African Renaissance
Vol. 4 No.1 Quarter 1 2007
pp10-19

Ethiopia: A hegemony of a minority group is unstable and undemocratic

Berhanu Gutema Balcha

Introduction

Ethnicity and federalism have become the major factors in organizing the political and territorial space in Ethiopia since 1991. The Tigrayan People's Liberation Front (TPLF), which had started its movement for the liberation of its ethnic territory from the central Ethiopian administration, has advocated ethnic- federalism, vowing to equalize the diverse ethnic communities. As a result, the overall centralized structure of the previous regime has been replaced by a 'federal' system consisting of nine ethnically and regionally delimited regional states and the Addis Ababa city administration.

The 'ethnic- federal' experiment of devolving public sector powers to ethnic groups goes against the centralized nation-building project of the previous regimes. The previous regimes used a different model; they gave much emphasis to 'Ethiopian nationalism' as a unifying concept and promoted centralization rather than regional or ethnic autonomy.

The TPLF and the Tigrayan elite would have lost their privileged position with a genuine ethnic federal arrangement in Ethiopia.

The rule of the emperor was based on absolutism and concentration of power on the king himself through a patrimonial network of power, resource and privilege accumulation and distribution system that benefits the rulers and their few collaborators at local, regional and central levels. The major orientation of the imperial state was to use the state power for voracious appropriation of resources, mainly from the peasantry, in order to reward the few ruling nobilities, viceroy and their clienteles that maintain the survival of the highly centralised state. Although the brutality of appropriation and mode of domination differ from place to place due to the historical process and mode of incorporation into the centralized state structure, the expansion toward the south accompanied with the assertion of cultural superiority of the Orthodox Christian core and the serfdom and exploitation of the people of the south (Clapham 2002: 10, Teshale 1995: 176, Bahiru 1994, Messay 1999). In the process, many of the southern Ethiopian peasantry were turned into serfs in their own land when the 'ownership' of their land was transferred to the emperor, nobilities and loyal followers of the imperial authority. Though the predatory state had showed some favouritism based on provincial ethnicity for functional purpose, it promoted 'state nationalism' and 'national integration' with the perception of national identity as the mirror-image of the *Shoan* ruling elite's ethnic and cultural manifestations such as Amharic language, Orthodox Christianity, self-proclaimed moral superiority and military triumph over others. It is indisputable that language proficiency plays a significant role in determining better access to education and employment by putting in a relatively disadvantageous situation those groups whose language is not used in employment and education

The military regime, after 1974, repeatedly stressed that it preferred 'socialist' solution to the nationalities question but promoted militaristic nationalism by means of authoritarian and highly centralized political system. It initiated, however, few measures like broadcasting radio programmes in Afar, Somali, *Oromiffa* and *Tigrgna* languages, establishing national research institution for studying nationalities and drawing a new internal boundary based on ethno-territorial bases. It also made a radical shift in landownership in 1975, particularly in the southern part of Ethiopia, by destroying the exploitative and unjust land appropriation of the nobility and others. Although the radical change abolished serfdom by distributing the land to the peasants, land remained the property of the state and thus made the peasantry highly intervened and controlled by the state. Nevertheless, it did not make any attempt to link ethnic rights with politics or governance issues. Rather without any regional or ethnic prejudices, it imposed its greater centralization and brutal governance system, controlled at the core by junior military officers regardless of their ethnic affiliation or orientations. Militaristic state nationalism, blended with socialism, was promoted in the hope of obliterating regional and ethnic movements. However, excessive centralization backed by ruthless coercion did not abate regional and ethnic movements. Rather, it exacerbated internal turmoil and massive resentment by the population, which provided a good opportunity for the expansion of ethnonational movements that finally overran the state's centre in 1991 by defeating the military regime, and introducing politics of ethnic autonomy and ethnic entitlement.

Ethnicity: a theoretical challenge and empirical nuisance

Structuring of society and politics on the basis of ethnicity has been viewed by many scholars as a risky approach for the reason that politicisation of ethnicity could excessively awaken ethnic consciousness and unleash ethnic groupings at the expense of shared identities and interspersed settlements (Horowitz 1985, Messay 1999, Clapham 2002). It is held that ethnic entitlements could give much more leverage to blood relationships and ascriptive loyalties in place of rights and duties (Kedourie 1993). It could also promote the rule of kin, instead of the rule of law, because ascribed ethnic solidarity is viewed as more important than merit and other achieving qualities in the ideology of ethnic entitlement, therefore sharing the same genealogy will be a reassurance for assuming political leadership. Ethnic entitlement can also be used by ethnic leaders to gather justification or legitimisation for autocratic rule in the name of their ethnic community. Ali A. Mazrui also asserts that the preponderance of affinitive or kinship ties within societies would pose formidable barriers in building tolerant multiethnic societies (Ali. A. Mazrui 1967).

The hegemonic ambition of the Tigrayan elite or the TPLF has been the major factor in blocking an effective power-sharing federal government in Ethiopia.

On the other hand, scholars concerned about ethnically fragmented societies suggest that in order to reduce ethnic tensions and conflicts, it is imperative for multiethnic states to engineer accommodative structure in order to achieve peaceful coexistence(O'Leary 2002, Lijphart 1994; 2002). A prominent scholar in the field of ethnicity, politics and power-sharing in multiethnic societies, Arend Lijphart (1994) urges the designing of ethnic power sharing arrangements or consociational model in segmented or divided societies. According to Arend Lijphart the successful political accommodation of diverse ethnic groups could be achieved through recognition and devising appropriate institutions for accommodation and power sharing. In his discussion of consociational politics, Lijphart enumerated four necessary institutional arrangements in accommodating diversities. These are power sharing government (grand coalition), mutual veto, proportionality and segmental autonomy (Lijphart 1977). In his discussion Lijphart outlined the necessity to have proportional representation from all significant groups, a protection for minority groups, and a territorial autonomy or non-territorial division of power or functional autonomy. Although Lijphart's consociational democracy is criticized for its high reliance on the good will of elites, it can be used as a model for engineering appropriate institutional structures in places where diverse ethnic groups are competing and fighting for controlling the state power.

In line with Lijphart's argument other scholars suggest also that stability in culturally fragmented countries increases if these countries adopt a political system characterised by proportionality, grand coalition, federalism and strong veto points (Steiner et al 2003: 82). Ethnic federalism is suggested as a relatively preferable institutional arrangement in case of geographically concentrated ethnic groups. Federalism can provide an autonomous space for power exercise and a space for expression for territorially concentrated homogeneous ethnic groups. In such case it could reduce demands for separation and other tensions associated with secession.

However, scholars like Donald Horowitz (1985 & 2002) and Basta Fleiner (2000) argue that ethnic arrangement as a means to ensure ethnic self-government could further radicalise ethnic problem by turning ethnic demands into political principles rather than providing a remedy or cure. In this connection, federal framework based on ethnic coalition could be a very unstable form of government, because ethnic elites could be possessed by their own sectional self-interest to pull apart the framework or the coalition. They could also be constrained by their ethnic community if they concede much for the sake of cooperation. Horowitz (2002) therefore argues that federalism should aim to create an integrative dynamics by encouraging ethnically heterogeneous groups or political units to work together within a shared structure that can provide incentives for inter-ethnic co-operation. For Horowitz, non-ethnic federal units could help to forge common interests, other than ethnic identities, among people living within the same federal units in order to compete against the other federal units beyond ethnic interests. Horowitz believes that the remedy for ethnic problem is institutionalisation of 'ethnically blind' structures and policies that could reduce or undermine ethnic divide. However, he recognises that in a climate of elite competition 'a fear of ethnic domination and suppression is a motivating force for the acquisition of power as an end and it is also sought for confirmation of ethnic status' (Horowitz 1985: 187). 'An ethnic contrast that has produced an extraordinary amount of conflict in many African, Asian, and Caribbean states is the juxtaposition of 'backward' and 'advanced' groups' (Horowitz 1985: 148). Thus, Horowitz advises that 'if indeed ethnicity and ethnic organisations provide security to groups in an uncertain environment, then attempts to replace or outlaw them may have the effect of increasing insecurity' (Horowitz 1985: 567-8). It could be essential, therefore, to recognise the importance of power-sharing and territorial devolution. Territorial compartmentalization with devolution of generous power can have tranquillising effects in countries with territorially separate groups, significant sub-ethnic divisions and serious conflict at the centre (Horowitz 1985: 614). It is very vital to consider the importance of timing in engineering a political process and structure, because 'accommodation long delayed may be accommodation ultimately denied' (Horowitz 1985: 617).

As Walker Connor (1999) articulates, ethnonational movements' are found worldwide, they

'... are to be found in Africa (for example, Ethiopia), Asia (Sri Lanka), Eastern Europe (Romania), Western Europe (France), North America (Guatemala), South America (Guyana), and Oceania (New Zealand). The list includes countries that are old (United Kingdom), as well as new (Bangladesh), large (Indonesia), as well as small (Fiji), rich (Canada), as well as poor (Pakistan), authoritarian (Sudan) as well as democratic (Belgium), Marxist-Leninist (China) as well as militantly anti-Marxist (Turkey). The list also includes countries which are Buddhist (Burma), Christian (Spain), Moslem (Iran), Hindu (India) and Judaic (Israel). (Connor 1999: 163-4).

Ethnic associations and ethnic parties have been discouraged and banned in many countries and in majority cases due to fear of the presumed radical and destructive backlashes of ethnic demands and ethnic rights. Vindictive horrors of ethnic conflicts, genocide and ethnic cleansing in cases like Rwanda, former Yugoslavia and Nigeria and also relatively less but unrelenting and destructive ethnic strives in places such as Sudan, India, Malaysia, Sri Lanka and others are signalling the recalcitrant nature of ethnic demands and also indicating the difficult challenges connected to ethnic entitlement and ethnic rights.

However, in his cross-national study of communal based conflicts, Ted Gurr (1994) shows that 'ethnic identity and interest per se do not risk unforeseen ethnic wars; rather, the danger is hegemonic elites who use the state to promote their own people's interest at the expense of others (Gurr 2000: 64). Thus, he warns that 'the push of state corruption and minority repression probably will be a more important source of future ethnic wars than the 'pull' of opportunity' (Ibid). Horowitz also asserts that even if ethnic problems are intractable, they are not altogether without hope; 'even in the most severely divided societies, ties of blood do not lead to ineluctably to rivers of blood' (Ibid. p. 682). Power-sharing and coalition political frameworks that could encourage inter-ethnic cooperation by ensuring recognition of some prominent group's rights could be one option to minimise group's resentments and mitigate destructive conflicts.

A paradox in Ethiopia: a tiny minority poor region demands and monopolises federalism

In the Ethiopian context, the TPLF was inherently and structurally deficient to embark on establishing a genuine accommodative political framework. The TPLF officially and proudly claims to represent the Tigray province and the Tigray people. The Tigray people constitute only six percent of the total population of Ethiopia, a very tiny minority in Ethiopia's ethnic configuration when compared to the Oromo and Amhara people that represent about 35 and 30 per cent of the Ethiopian people respectively. The Tigray province has been the most impoverished, environmentally degraded and relatively highly vulnerable to frequent draught and famine. Without siphoning or supplementing resource from the other parts of Ethiopia, it is unlikely that the province could sustain the current, though still precarious, life standard. Conceivably, therefore the TPLF's ethnic empowerment discourse could damage more the interest and benefit of the Tigray elite and the TPLF, if it is to be implemented genuinely. The TPLF and the Tigrayan elite would have lost their privileged position with a genuine ethnic federal arrangement in Ethiopia.

As a result, the TPLF was not interested to create a genuine ethnic coalition government and a genuine ethnic federal arrangement in Ethiopia that would certainly put it in a gravely disadvantageous position. More importantly, the Tigray province, a home of the TPLF, would be the least to be benefited from a genuine federal arrangement in Ethiopia, therefore it may not wish for a federal arrangement. Consequently, the intention of the TPLF has been a sham federal arrangement through a superficial ethnic coalition arrangement. It has been embarking on sustaining a political travesty via EPRDF (Ethiopian Peoples' Revolutionary Democratic Force) that would assure its hegemonic project by using ethnic rights as a discourse to attract ethnic elites.

Ethnic rights and ethnic entitlement have become an attractive inducement for many of the elites from various ethnic groups to fall so easily into the trap of the TPLF's manipulation and machination. Many surrogate elites, who did not have any legitimacy from their respective ethnic communities, have become instruments of the TPLF's hegemonic desire, as they were easily susceptible to TPLF's rewarding or/and coercing power. In this case, the TPLF has been consistent in its core policy of promoting first and foremost the interests of the Tigray elite. As Merera claims, 'the ultimate goal has been to ensure the centrality of Tigrayan elite in the reordering of the Ethiopian State and society' (Merera 2002: 119).

The hegemonic ambition of the Tigrayan elite or the TPLF has been the major factor in blocking an effective power-sharing federal government in Ethiopia. From the beginning, the TPLF/EPRDF dominated the constitutional drafting process and the procedures for establishing an elected government that replaced the transition government. The TPLF was more interested in promoting its project of reasserting the hegemony the Tigray nationalism in Ethiopia. The Tigrayan elites have been very nostalgic about the past glory and standing of Tigray in the history of the Ethiopian state (Aregawe 2004: 576). Marcus states that 'Tigrayan felt marginalized by their Christian Amhara cousins, even though the Tigray had participated in Emperor Menelik's empire building and in Emperor Haile Selassie's effort to establish a nation' (Marcus 2002: 221). Kinfe Abreha argues that 'the Tigrians also resent the unfair historical process through which the Tigrians' overlordship of Emperor Yohannes IV was lost to Menelik II, leading to the gradual decline of the region from the citadel of the Empire' to a quasi autonomous one' (Kinfe 1994: 159). He writes that: 'The Tigray resistance is naturally the outcome of the gradual decline of the region whose human and material potentials was spent in the preservation of the territorial integrity of Ethiopia. It was the case of a candle that consumed itself while giving light to its surroundings' (Ibid.). Adhana also claims that Tigray, defined by its predominant Christian character, formed not only a durable component of the Ethiopian nation but was also part of the backbone of the Ethiopian state and thus 'everything that defined the Ethiopian state was a result of Aksumite invention and innovation.' (Adhana 1998: 43). These assertions may reflect the disquiet of the Tigrayan elite on lost pride due to 'a humiliating sense of exclusion from the important centre of power'.

Although many critics have accused the TPLF of excessively empowering ethnic groups, the real practice has been that the TPLF has co-opted elites from the various ethnic groups who did not make an effective resistance against the dominance of the Tigrayan elite in the Ethiopian state. Here, the most important point to understand is that the TPLF/EPRDF has not been an honest force in implementing a genuine ethnic federalism. Actually, the TPLF is not giving a real power to the ethnic communities, but is promoting surrogate elites and ethnic entrepreneurs from various ethnic communities who have facilitated the expansion of its influence and rule in their respective areas. The implication is that the ethnic federal arrangement has been used by the TPLF in order to extend its authority beyond its own territory so as to make the Tigrayan elite a dominant political and economic force in the Ethiopian state.

Although the TPLF claims that it has been struggling, first and foremost, for the rights of the Tigrayan people for self-determination, its legitimacy in Tigray has not been confirmed democratically. Nevertheless, it is evident that the TPLF has been able to secure immense moral and political support from some section of the people of Tigray because of its 'commitment' to the reassertion and promotion of Tigrayan nationalism. It is becoming clear that the ethnic federal arrangement in Ethiopia has been used by the TPLF to establish the hegemony of the Tigray nationalism over other nationalisms, including the 'Ethiopian nationalism'. Though it is difficult to know whether the Tigrean people as a whole support or benefit from the strategy of the TPLF, there is ample evidence that the Tigrayan elites have been benefiting significantly in getting dominant political and economic positions, which are disproportionate to the share they should have been given in accordance with the ethnic entitlement principles of the dicta of ethnic federalism in Ethiopia.

According to the principles of its own ideology of fair and equal representation of ethic groups, the TPLF, which represents the Tigray province with its six percent of the Ethiopian population, should have assumed a minority role, if its intention has not been an ethnic hegemony via ethnic federalism. But, because it has operated contrary to the rule of its own game, the TPLF is behaving like an instrument of coercion and domination rather than equality and freedom. As a result, the ethnic federal arrangement in Ethiopia has been characterised by armed domination and brutal suppression. In a nutshell, the ethnic federal project in Ethiopia has become a device for the implementation and protection of the hegemonic position of the tiny minority Tigrayan elites who desire to have a dominant control of resources that the Ethiopian state controls and generates.

Conclusion

There would be no magic democratic formula or military adventure that can make the TPLF or the Tigrayan elite a majority group in present day Ethiopia. A continuation of brutal and forceful rule by a minority rule group could in long run lead to a chaotic scenario in which the majority may rise to take a desperate violent action to free themselves from the despotism of a minority group. It is totally unfeasible and unsustainable for a small minority ethnic group to assume a hegemonic and leadership position in a context where the consciousness of the people as well as of the ethnic communities is sufficiently mature to distinguish between what is appropriate and what is not. Military force and other deceptive strategies such as co-option of elites and, divide and rule tactics may work for some time, but such strategies can not create a genuine framework that can nurture a workable political system in a sustainable way. The TPLF is getting considerable support from the US because of its tactical alliance in the 'coalition of the willing' and the 'war on terror', however, it is unwise to rely on external patron in a sustainable manner. Neither the imperial rule, nor the military regime was saved by its external patron. It is evident that the willingness of the people to accept the rule of the TPLF/EPRDF has been weakening. The May 2005 Ethiopian election, in which the TPLF/EPRDF forcefully changed the outcome of the election's result (as reported by the European Union's Election observers mission and by all civil society groups in Ethiopia), was a clear message from the Ethiopian people to the TPLF that the Ethiopians are badly in need of a democratic change and they are also ready to make it happen.

References

Adhana H. Adhana 1998. 'Tigray- The Birth of a Nation within the Ethiopian Polity'. In Mohammed Salih, M. A. and J. Markakis (eds.) *Ethnicity and the State in Eastern Africa.* Uppsala: Nordiska Afrikaninstituten.

Aregawi Berhe 2004. 'THE ORIGINS OF THE TIGRAY PEOPLE'S LIB-ERATION FRONT', *in African Affairs* (2004), 103/413, pp 569–592, Royal

African Society

Bahiru Zewde 1991. *History of Modern Ethiopia 1855-1974,* Addis Ababa: Addis Ababa University

Clapham, Christopher 2002. *Controlling Space in Ethiopia* in James, Wendy, Donham, Donald L., Kurimoto, Eisei, and Triulzi, Alessandro. (Eds.) *Remapping Ethiopia.* London: James Currey.

Connor, Walker 1999. 'National Self-determination and Tomorrow's Political Map'. In

Alan Cairns (ed.) *Citizenship, Diversity and Pluralism.* Montreal: McGill Queen's University Press.

Fleiner, Lidija R. Basta 2000. 'Can Ethnic Federalism Work?'- Paper for the Conference On "Facing Ethnic Conflicts", Bonn, Germany 14-16, December 2000 - Center for Development Research (ZEF Bonn).

Gurr, T. Robert 2000 'Ethnic Warfare on the Wane' in *Foreign Affairs,* May/June 2000, Volume 79, Number 3, pp 52 - 64

Horowitz, Donald L. 1985. *Ethnic Groups in Conflict.* Berkeley, Los Angeles, and London: University of California Press)

----------------------- 2002. Constitutional Design: Proposals versus Processes. In Andrew Reynolds *(ed.), The Architecture of Democracy, Constitutional Design, Conflict Management, and Democracy.* Oxford: Oxford University Press

Kedourie, Elie 1993. *Nationalism.* London: Hutchinson

Kinfe, Abraham 1994. *Ethiopia from Bullets to the Ballot Box.* NJ: The Red Sea Press

Lijphart, Arend 1977. *Democracy in Plural Societies.* New Haven: Yale University Press

------------------ 1994. 'Prospects for Power-Sharing in the New South Africa' *in Reynolds*A. (ed.) Election '94 South Africa: The Campaigns, Results and Future Prospects. Oxford: Oxford University Press.

------------------ 2002. 'The Wave of Power-Sharing Democracy' in Andrew Reynolds (ed.) *The Architecture of Democracy: Constitutional Design, Conflict Management, and Democracy.* Oxford: Oxford University Press.

Marcus, Harold 2002. *A History of Ethiopia.* Berkeley: University of California Press

Mazrui, Ali A. 1967. *Soldiers and Kinsmen in Uganda: The making of a MilitaryEthnocracy.* Beverly Hills: Sage

Merera Gudina 2003. *Ethiopia: Competing ethnic nationalisms and the quest fordemocracy,* 1960 – 2000. PhD dissertation.

Messay Kebede 1999. *Survival and Modernisation: Ethiopia's Enigmatic Present: A Philosophical Discourse.* New Jersey and Asmara: The Red Sea Press, Inc.

O'Leary, Brendan, 2002. 'Federations and the Management of nations: Agreement and arguments with Walker Connor and Ernest Gellner'. In Daniele Conversi (ed.) *Ethnonationalism in the Contemporary World: Walker Connor and the study of nationalism,* London and New York: Routledge. pp

153-183

Steiner Jürg, André Bächtiger, Markus Spörndli, Marco R. Steenbergen, 2003. *Deliberative politics in action: Crossnational study of parliamentary debates.* Cambridge: Cambridge University Press

Gurr, T. Robert and Barbara Harff, 1994. *Ethnic Conflict in World Politics.* Oxford, Boulder, and San Francisco: Westview Press

Teshale Tibebu 1995. *The Making of Modern Ethiopia 1896 – 1974.* NJ: Red Sea Press

---

Berhanu Gutema Balcha is at Aalborg UniversityResearch Centre for Development and International Relations:
Email: berhanu@ihis.aau.dk

African Journal of Business and Economic Research

AJBER

Annual Subscription Rates

Companies/orgs./institutions:	£200
(including access to the online editions)	
Individuals: hardcopy only:	£50
Individuals: online and Print:	£60
Individuals: Online only:	£30
Retail sales:	
Individuals (print)	£20 (+ P&P)
Online	£10 per issue

For subscription and advertisement enquiries contact:

sales@adonis-abbey.com
Phone: +44 (0) 20 7793 8893

Adonis & Abbey Publishers Ltd
P.O. Box 43418,
London
SE11 4XZ
United Kingdom

African Renaissance
Vol. 4 No.1 Quarter 1 2007
pp22-27

Somalia and The End of Mogadishu Syndrome?

Mohamed Haji Mukhtar

The fall of Mogadishu on New Year's Eve to the allied forces of the Transitional Federal Government (TFG) and Ethiopia won't hurt the Union of Islamic Court's (UIC) jihad in Ethiopia, nor will it automatically bring stability to war- torn Somalia. It is unlikely that the UIC will lay down their arms and surrender their militias, or that the TFG will be able to extend its authority outside of Mogadishu. This is the general opinion among many Somalis and friends of Somalia, largely because Somalia's past 16 years have shown so many tangible examples of unsustainable transitions.

However, this latest transition could be an opportunity to close a chapter of instability and anarchy in the Somali peninsula. If successful, it may bring the end of lawlessness and of Somalia's stigma as the only failed state on the globe. In the longer run, it may help to restore the unity of Somalia and to curb the war on global terror.

Since the collapse of the state in January 1991, Mogadishu has experienced a number of disastrous transitional authorities which have left their mark on the Somali psyche as well as on that of the international community. During Ali Mahdi's interim government (1991-92), the city was turned into rubble because of indiscriminate shellings between Mahdi's militia and rival forces led by Muhamad Farah Aideed. Mogadishu was divided by a defacto "Green Line", where Mahdi's militia controlled the northern portion of the city and Aideed's the southern.[i] The post-Arta settlements of May-August, 2000, brought about the Transitional National Government (TNG) with Abdulqasim Salad Hassan as President.[ii] The TNG could not establish its authority over even one sector of Mogadishu. Then the Mbeghathi[iii] Peace and Reconciliation Conference of 2002-2004 produced the Transitional Federal Government (TFG). The new president Abdullahi Yusuf Ahmed and the majority members of his parliament failed even to "put their feet" in Mogadishu because of fears for their security. Now after more than two years of brief sojourns in Jowhar (2005) and Baidoa (2006), the TFG has taken over Mogadishu with Ethiopian support and without resistance. The UIC who controlled the city from June 2006 withdrew and their leaders are on the run.

For the past 16 years, Mogadishu's residents have lived under different reigns of terror. More than 10 warlords split the city into enclaves. Their "isbaro," checkpoints, limited the mobility of the local residents as well as the flow of goods and services. Each enclave controlled aspects of the city's security and economic resources i.e. ports, airports, airstrips and leading roads to the rest of the country. Since 1990 all attempts to establish an autonomous administration for Mogadishu city have failed. The city became a safe haven for criminals. Assassinations of Somali peacemakers, educators, medical doctors as well as international humanitarian providers were common; victims included Mohamud Ali Ahmed Elman (March 1997), Ayub Sheikh Yerow Abdiyow (September 19, 1999), Abdulqadir Yahya (July, 2005); and Dan Eldon (1993), Sister Leonella Sgorbati (2006), and Kate Payton of the BBC (February 9, 2006). In June, 1993, it was in Mogadishu where dozens of UN peacekeepers were murdered while guarding an outside soup kitchen for the malnourished and victims of the famine.[iv] Moreover, the massacre of Black Hawk Dawn cost 18 US troops in Operation Restore Hope their lives (1993).[v] Somalis in general and Mogadishans in particular were murdering the very individuals or groups who were attempting to help them.

It is obvious that Somalis failed to help themselves and recover from the abyss, and the international communities seemed unable to tackle the root causes of the problem. Somalia needed to root out weapons and militias or faction leaders in order to promote reconciliation and effective governance. Unfortunately, efforts towards disarmament failed during the past 16 years. There are a number of lessons to be learned from Somalia's past, when the country was devastated by similar crises. In the post World War I era, 1923-27, armed Somalis returning from the war zones started vandalizing the region. The Italian administration succeeded in "pacifying" them and controlling a territory even vaster than Somalia today (called "la Grande Somalia" - the greater Somalia) by introducing a serious policy of disarmament.[vi] Similarly, after World War II, the British Military Administration (BMA), 1941-50, faced the same question. The defeat of Italy in the Horn of Africa by the Allied Forces left Somalia in a political vacuum, because Italy had earlier destroyed the Somali lines of authority. Moreover, thousands of young Somalis armed by the Italians were left behind with their weapons. These young men, mostly recruited from the nomadic clans turned the country into a scene of pillage and plunder. The BMA had no clear mandate to govern Somalia. Its responsibility was a transitional one, to keep Somalia as an "Occupied Enemy Territory" until the Allies –the Four Powers- decided the future of such areas, but the situation gave new incentives to the Somali pastoral propensity for property looting and inter-clan feuds. The BMA had no other choice but to disarm the Somalis.[vii] While the means and goals of the colonial powers in

Somalia were not precisely the same as those of today's multinational troops, the circumstances and clan intrigues of the Somalis are quite similar.

For example, when inter-clan war spread throughout the country and caused a famine in the inter-riverine region in 1991-93, the U.S. led Operation Restore Hope (ORH) was essential to keep Somalia's brigands and their weapons at bay while relief aid was being delivered. During the United Nations Operation in Somalia (UNOSOM) which followed ORH, Somalia began a tentative recovery. Baidoa, which the media in 1992 had called "the City of Walking Dead," reclaimed its historic name "Baidoa Jinay" the heavenly city; and the inter-riverine region that was labeled as "the Triangle of Death" became one of the most peaceful regions of the country.[viii] However, immediately after the withdrawal of the international authority ORH and UNOSOM, new forms of anarchic authority emerged in the region. The Republic of Somaliland which had seceded in1991 was joined by the autonomous Riverine State in Baidoa (formed in March 1995, and overthrown by Aideed in September, 1995) and by the regional authority of Puntland State in Garowe in 1998. Thus, Somalia went back to square one.

Operation Restore Hope and UNOSOM will be remembered widely as a success story in Somali history. The missions alleviated an unimaginable tragedy among the devastated Somalis. But its success would have been more lasting if the rescued Somalis had been helped towards a workable political solution in a parallel effort to the humanitarian cause, and if the international community had been more aware of the real causes behind the Somali tragedy.

Recent examples also might shed some light on the necessity of international intervention in Somalia's affairs. Since leaving Nairobi in November 2004, the TFG failed to achieve a quorum for a meeting. Some of the TFG parliamentarians went to Mogadishu, arguing that the seat of the government should return to the old capital, while others refused to go Mogadishu believing it could not provide the necessary security. They agreed instead on Jowhar, 90km North of Mogadishu as an interim capital until Mogadishu was secure. None of the groups could have a quorum and this kept the TFG dysfunctional for over a year. In February, 2006, the two groups agreed to convene in Baidoa, 250km West of Mogadishu. This would have been impossible without UN facilitation. The UNDP provided some basic operational funds, including infrastructures, services and some basic security.

On 28 February, 2006, the 275 members of the parliament convened and called for the necessity of international involvement in Somalia.[ix] It became clear that the TFG would remain handicapped without international assistance. No progress whatsoever could be achieved without rigorous deployment of international troops to tackle the issue of disarmament, which is essential to sustainable peace and reconciliation in the country. It is also obvious that without stability no meaningful reconstruction is possible and all social and economic progress will remain doomed.

The TFG invited the international community to take action, this time not to rescue Somali people from famine or to restore its failed state, but rather to prop up the faltering government and prevent the establishment of a Taliban-style state that might provide a safe haven for al-Qaeda and other terrorist groups in Somalia. The African Union (AU) authorized deployment of troops for this endeavor.[x] Ethiopia was the first to heed the call, initially providing trainers and more recently sizeable numbers of troops, following the UIC attacks on Baidoa, the headquarters of the TFG. The UIC are backed militarily by Eritrea and Egypt, the archrival of Ethiopia in the Horn of Africa, financed by Iran and Saudi Arabia, and has the overwhelming support of global jihad movement. In Baidoa the UIC staged some serious suicide bombings. In September, 2006, Abdullahi Yusuf Ahmed president of the TFG, survived from a devastating attack where eight of his bodyguards were killed. Baidoa also experienced some heinous assassinations. In July, 28, 2006 Abdalla Derow Issaq, Minister of Federal Affairs, and other dignitaries were shot at point blank range; the assassins were never captured. These are just some example of al-Qaeda style actions in Baidoa. In Mogadishu and elsewhere where the Islamists established control since June 2006, they introduced practices that are antithetical to Islamic values such as chopping off hands of thieves or generally applying "hudud" laws when there is no functioning state apparatus; laws forbidding women from riding in cars with men even when there is no transportation capable of supporting that segregation; and introduced regulations that men cannot shave beards or watch television. No women were included in their Shura and Executive Councils.

The UIC showed themselves to be insensitive about Islam in the Horn of Africa. Almost half of Ethiopia's population professes Islam and most of the times live harmoniously with the other Christian half. This is true with Eritrea as well. If the Somali Islamists are in the pursuit of establishing an Islamic state they should have been passionate about Ethiopia's legacy on Islam. When companions of the Prophet Muhammad were persecuted by their own clansman, the Meccans, the Prophet suggested that they to go to "Abyssinia": there "¼ you will find a king under whom none are persecuted. It is land of righteousness¼" Indeed, the companions were given asylum and safe haven and were protected from Meccan retrieval.[xi] It is believed that Islam came to Somalia from this migration. And Somalis are proud of claiming that they became Muslims even before Medina.

The outcome of the Ethiopian interventions and the eventual empowerment of the TFG should be looked at by both Somalis and the international community as a potential blessing in disguise. Somalia lacked governance for the past 16 years, and it is ranked the bottom of development index. The masses have been yearning to have their state back to have some semblance of dignity. Now that the TFG is functional, Somalis should welcome and work towards the success of the TFG. The armed Somalis are the problem. For a sustainable peace and stability, they must voluntarily give up their guns. It would have been ideal to disarm without foreign intervention. Somalis should first and foremost do their homework. Building roads, schools, hospital and other basic civic infrastructure would be impossible if builders are at gun point or infrastructure are bombed at any moment. The Somali people should put down arms and the government should find alternatives for the armed youth. We need to give peace a chance.

The international community should commit itself more than ever. Multinational troops must be deployed immediately, first for helping the disarmament process in 6 months, and then for training the Somali police force in a year. The task of reconciliation and reconstruction is more than Ethiopia can do alone. In fact the continued presence of Ethiopian troops in Somalia would inflame tensions. Genuine reconciliation should start and grievances should settle. It is necessary to bring the war criminals to justice. It took Liberia many years to nail Charles Tailor. After Taylor was indicted, not only Liberia, but many countries of North West Africa were able to restore piece. Similarly, The Democratic Republic of Congo is expected to be at peace after putting the infamous warlord Thomas Lubanga in the International Criminal Court's custody. The international community must ban Somali warlords, and islamicists alleged to have ties with international terrorism from coming to their countries –stop issuing visas- and freeze and shut down their bank accounts. This opportunity may not last long. The UIC may be retreating for tactical reason, and though they have restricted freedoms, they brought some degree of stability not seen before in Somalia. If the TFG cannot bring about better stability and tangible progress in the near future, this might invite insurgencies and the Somali crises could overflow and turn the entire region into a battlefield, and Somalia might descend to chaos again.

References

[i] John L. Hirsch and Robert B. Oakley, Somalia and Operation Restore Hope: Reflections on Peacemaking and Peacekeeping (Washington, DC: United States Institute of Peace), pp. 14-16.

[ii] Arta is a summar resort in Djibouti where the reconciliation conference was held. See details in Mohamed Haji Mukhtar, Historical Dictionary of Somalia, New Edition (Lanham, MD: Scarecrow Press, 2003), pp. 41-42.

[iii] Another resort in Kenya.

[iv] John Drysdale, "Foreign Military Intervention in Somalia: The Root

Cause of the Shift From UN Peacekeeping and its Consequences." In *Learning From Somalia: The Lessons of Armed Humanitarian Intervention*, edited by Walter Clarke and Jeffery Herbst (Boulder, Colorado: Westview Pres, 1997), p. 132.

[v] Mark Bowden, *Black Hawk Down: A Story of Modern War*, (New York: Atlantic Monthly Press, 1999), pp. 261-326.

[vi] De Vecchi di Val Cismon, *Orizzonti d'Impero (Cinque Anni in Somalia)*. (Milan: A. Mondadori), pp. 25-27.

[vii] E. Sylvia Pankhurst, *Ex-Italian Somaliland* (New York: Philosophical Library, 1951), pp. 164-169.

[viii] Mohamed Haji Mukhtar, "The Plight of Agro-Pastoral Society of Somalia." *Review of African Political Economy*, Vol. 23, No. 70, (1996), p. 552.

[ix] Crisis Group Africa Report No. 116, *Can The Somali Crisis be Contained?* August 10, 2006, pp. 7-8.

[x] In January 2005, leaders of the Inter-Governmental Authority on Development IGAD authorized the deployment of a peace support mission known as IGASOM to help the TFG on disarming militias, training police force and maintain law and order in the country.

[xi] Abi Muhammad Abdulmalik Ibn Hisham al-Ma'afiri, *Al-Sirah al-Nabawiyyah*, Vol. 1, (Cairo: Dar al-Hadith, 1996), pp. 266-281.

Dr. Mohamed Haji Mukhtar, is a Professor of African and Middle Eastern

AK

African Renaissance
Vol. 4 No.1 Quarter 1 2007
pp28-34

The Horn of Africa: A reflection on the Christmas War on Somalia and its aftermath

Osman Farah and Mammo Muchie

Background analysis of the Horn of Africa

The Horn of Africa is awash with various types of deadly weapons, fuelled through endless conflicts rooted in the period of the European Scramble for Africa (indeed if not earlier!) to the period of de-colonisation in the 60s and throughout the post-colonial period. The region has been a victim of the arms race sponsored largely, if not exclusively, and distributed by the ex-colonial powers and the Cold War super powers, who did a classic swap for Ethiopia and Somalia during the 1977-78 War! The region does have the capability to use modern deadly weapons that could cost millions of lives. In certain occasions rulers in the region received these weapons as an integrated part of the development aid from major powers. Warlords, for instance those in Somalia, used to purchase the weapons from the numerous open capitalist markets in and around some Western and Eastern European countries. To the surprise of many, some of the notorious warlords in Mogadishu, as late as last year terrorised innocent civilians with new weapons imported from the UK, a western country that officially supports the UN weapons embargo against Somalia. Thus, the flow of weaponry and easy accessibility appears to constitute one of the main challenges to peace and stability in the Horn of Africa. Other serious obstacles include the prevailing divisive political culture and the colonial legacy.

European colonial powers as far back as the Portuguese and later, British, Italian and French have shown greater interest in the strategic importance of the Horn of Africa region. These powers exploited and manipulated the region in dividing the countries between themselves. Many of the recurring upheavals the countries in the region confront go back to the history of external subordination. Even Ethiopian kings that were accused of allying with European powers suffered under this dictation.

Then the cold war geopolitical superpowers adversary came, expanding the armament race in the region and exacerbating conflicts. This provided ammunition and superiority to dictatorships that in the end paved the way for warlords, poverty, exodus, collapse or semi-collapse of the political and social infrastructure.

Somali Independence and the Aftermath

Since the independence of Somalia, Ethiopia and Somalia have had two major wars. The first took place in 1964, four years after Somalia got its independence from Britain and Italy. Officially, it started because of the Somali irredentism and claim of the Ogaden region. This is a semi desert region the British transferred to Ethiopia following the end of World War Two. Military analysts suggest that this war had no winner and loser. It provided hope for Somali nationalists that despite its recent establishment, the relatively infant age of the Somali army, they managed, somehow, to confront the much stronger Ethiopian army that at the time throughout Africa was referred to as the lions of Africa. In addition, it increased the confidence of the Somali army, eventually leading to the Somali army's subsequent accession of power in 1969. Subsequently receiving military aid from the Soviet Union and free oil from some Middle Eastern regimes, the dictatorial Barre regime confidently launched a surprise attack against Ethiopia in 1977. With free oil from Iraq and the Gulf, together with weapons from many countries, the Somali army captured a large portion of the Ogaden. Allies of then left-wing regime in Addis - Cuba, Yemen and the Soviets - that mysteriously switched sides led one year after the start of the war to the defeat of the Somali army. Returning to Somalia in disarray and demoralised, senior officers of the Somali army attempted a failed coup led by, among other officers, president of the current transitional federal Somali government, Abdullahi Yusuf Ahmed. Coup leaders that were captured were sentenced to death or sent to long term imprisonment.

Most researchers of Somalia agree that from this period, the Somali state began to decline while Barre began to consolidate his power through personal rule and clan division.

Dictatorship and rivalry

With the assistance and invitation of Mengistu, Abdullahi established an armed political opposition in Addis Ababa. In response, Siad Barre invited Ethiopian and Eritrean opposition groups, among them the current prime minister of Ethiopia, Meles Zenawi, and the Eritrean president, Isayyas Afeworki to build army and political bases in Mogadishu.

This ping-pong opposition engagement ended when Barre and Mengistu, with the mediation of Yemen, in 1990 agreed not to support each others' political and armed opposition groups. Somali opposition groups had no option but to take the war inside Somalia. The Somali national movement that represented the Northern part of Somali engaged in direct military conflict with the Siad Barre army in Somaliland. Abdullahi Yusuf's group began to attack central Somalia and Farah Aidid's group led militia attack on the capital and its surrounding regions.

From this perspective it is logical to suggest that the unexpected agreement between two of Horn of Africa's world known dictators hastened the start of devastating civil war in Somalia that still ravages the nation.

The Somali political system finally collapsed in 1991, after Barre fled and the subsequent entrance of Mogadishu by various unorganised conflicting warlords, mostly expelled from Ethiopia. Most of the world knows the rest of the history; starvation and human suffering, the intervention of the USA led troops to "restore hope" and later departure (1992- 1994) and the failed Unisom mission (1993-1995).

Somalia became the only country in the world that does not have a functioning political system. Even semi-collapsed systems such as Afghanistan and Liberia maintained a sort of government that operated in respective capitals.

The perception of Somalis of Ethiopia

Some Somalis consider Ethiopia as a sort of substitute of 'colonial power', which emerged as a potential hegemonic power in the region by acquiring and preserving historical alliance and relationship with major western colonial powers. The argument here is that Ethiopia was not torn asunder when colonial powers debated on the division, rule and exploitation of Africa. Ethiopia was under the Great-power pressure, but not a total victim to it, playing in fact to expand its territory at the same time as the European Scramble for Africa took place. In fact, following the end of the cold war, the Ethiopian king took over the role of Britain, in the case of Ogaden, which many Somalis consider as part of greater Somalia, as it was also able to arrange a federation with Eritrea with Great Power support. When the Ogaden was ceded to the Ethiopian king of the time, part of the pro- Somalia Foreign office in Britain was also supporting the Somali five star policies of bringing under one national flag all those in Somali inhabited territories. The seeds of war were planted at the same time as the terms of Somali's independence were debated. Britain's policy to cede the Ogaden on the one hand to the Ethiopian king, and support the Somali demand for a five star policy cannot be reconciled easily. War seems to be inevitable at the very time that the Somalis became eager to celebrate the birth of the Somali nation.

External interests and domestic actors have created the situation in the region from which there is still no clear exit route. Ethiopia, and particularly the Ethiopian people, have remained as much as the victims as the Somalis. The animosity that might exist between the two nations are manipulated and exacerbated by the additional needs of local dictators to prolong their tenure to rule and dictate over the people. The late prominent Somali poet, Abdulkadir Yam Yam and y leading Somali intellectuals belong to the group that sees both fraternal people as being victims of larger agendas pursued by the international ruling elites in syndicate with local ruling elites. In an opening ceremony in Addis Ababa in 1993, where Meles brought together warlords to Addis Ababa to form a government of national unity, Yam Yam declared the conflict between Somalia and Ethiopia formally concluded, describing Ethiopians as the leading nation of black people worldwide1.

Since that initial euphoric peace gathering in Addis, Ethiopia became deeply embroiled in Somalia, politically and militarily. As we know, the Meles regime in Addis has been characterised as an active member of the coalition of the willing. In other words Meles has joined the so- called global war on terror that has damaged the optimism of creating a better world in the 21st century by going for an exaggerated framing of world politics between those for terror and those against. This is the famous Bush doctrine for framing world politics. In reality the paradigm of the Cold War lives on. It is only one of the agents that dropped out, namely the former Soviet Union. In its place the world now has the terror networks that seem to be bolstered by the very fact that American power is used to 'fight' them.

Unilateral action, proxy wars and all other schemes of the Cold War are being reproduced without any restraint by any legal, moral and normative authority emanating from the UN system. The Meles regime, in alliance with the current US administration, claimed that they have a legitimate right to enter and hunt suspects in Somalia. In addition since the early nineties, Meles armed warlords and remained a vigorous participant in the fourteen or more peace processes to find solution for the Somali debacle. In the last peace conference held in Nairobi, Kenya that lasted two years, the regime in Addis remained master of this conference which the Somalis refer to as warlord conference in contrast to the Djibouti conference in 2000, which the Somalis regard as a proper forum for Civil Society gathering peace process. The IGAD, mainly Ethiopia government sponsored peace process in Nairobi, produced the current TNFG government led by warlords and clan members they selected for the transitional federal. This means that the current government has no internal legitimacy but enjoys, as it claims, international recognition. In order to rule a country you first need to secure an internal public legitimacy. More significantly, most of the individuals who are sitting in the government and the parliament represent the past (dictatorship and civil war) and not the future of Somalia where peace can prevail.

The Islamic religion plays a central role among the Somalis. Almost all the 10 million Somalis are Muslims. Somalis claim to have been converted to Islam even before the opening of Mecca and at the time of the creation of the first Islamic state in Medina, when Islam was under tremendous pressure, which led to the sending of delegation to seek refuge and help from the Abyssinian king. Thus Somalis do not differentiate Somalis from Islam.

The Rise of Islamic Union Courts

The Islamic Courts Union (ICU) emerged during the chaos of the civil war in 1990s. It came when clan groups, mainly in and around Mogadishu, organised themselves through religious lines primarily to protect their lives and property from thieves and warlords. In addition, they provided basic services and security for the vulnerable. When the USA, through its CIA office and embassy in Nairobi, invited and financed Mogadishu to establish anti-terrorism coalition to capture and deport suspected extremists, ICU group founded their own counter group to defend themselves. An armed conflict broke out in Mogadishu in February 2006 leading to the total defeat of warlords in May 2006 and the humiliation of the US.

In June 2006, with the equivalent of popular revolution, the ICU took over most of South Somalia, bringing in a short period of time some sort of stability that was absent in Somalia for a generation. Most of the world welcomed this development except the regime in Ethiopia and the US. The two countries remained sceptical of religious groups taking over total political and military power in Somalia. The UN and the Arab league attempted to bring the Somali parties together in Sudan, but these discussions failed because the ICU had their own vision of statehood, while the warlord-dominated government wanted to install a client government that would be an extended hand of the US and the regime in Addis. On their part some extreme elements in the ICU provided a pretext for the US and Ethiopia by formally declaring Jihad against Ethiopia if the Meles regime refused to withdraw its army from Somalia, which supported the TFG. Meles always maintained the existence of a terrorist threat in Somalia, and used the jihad by ICU as a pretext to send his forces into Somalia. The conventional Ethiopian army and air power, supported by US battle ships off the coast of Somalia providing intelligence, overpowered the ICU militia groups within weeks. The ICU claimed it was a tactical war retreat.

Consequently, the six months of ICU rule in South Somalia abruptly ended. The leadership fled towards the Kenyan border and the ICU militia appeared to have melted into the ordinary civilians waiting for a day they will possibly stage a come back.

Somali interpretation of current developments

Somalis are divided in their understanding and interpretation of these current dramatic developments. The optimists argue that African peace keeping troops will soon replace the Ethiopian forces and that for the first time in decades the rule of law will return to Somalia. They refer to the invasion of US during the Second World War in Japan and the invasion by Tanzania of Uganda to oust Ida Amin which both led to more stable and prosperous countries. They add that if people cannot put their house in order for so long, then they are entitled to be invaded and even ruled. The point is that Somalis have obviously chosen decades of anarchy and they cannot survive without outside help. Particularly minorities and women that suffered under dominance of major ruthless clans during the dark years of 1990s, welcome this external hegemonic involvement.

Others proclaim that the external invasion is yet another chapter of colonisation and that it will only strengthen the resistance and the unity of the Somali people. Sooner or later Somalis, they argue, will liberate their country from America and their allies.

There are also some who see the process as an integrated part of the global agenda led by the US against what is perceived to be a worldwide Muslim disaffection and unrest against the west and its values of freedom. This has intensified since September 11. Iraq, Afghanistan, Palestine and now Somalia are believed to be all part of the American effort to counter the threat it perceives as 'global terrorism.'

Ethiopia has been seen as a safe bet since it has a predominantly Christian population, though there are also as nearly as many Muslims as there are perhaps Christians. Ethiopia has been identified for waging a proxy war by neo-conservatives in the US. So, the Somali conflict is part of a global conflict. The aim is to prevent any other state forms, such as Islamic and indigenous African traditional forms, to emerge.

Possible scenarios

With regard to possible scenarios of the crises in the Horn, this is very difficult to predict. The worst case scenario will be if America and the regime in Addis continue to insist that the conflict in the Horn is part of the so-called global war against terrorism. Then prolonged suffering and hardship awaits the people in the region. There will be a war of religion and it will affect all countries in the region and beyond. Religious warlords will emerge.

The best outcome scenarios will be if the warlord-led government in Mogadishu engaged a process of civic inclusion where they invite all relevant political and social actors, including the leadership of ICU, to construct and find a comprehensive lasting solution to the Somali people and to the region as a whole.

The problem is that the warlord government does not have the vision and means to host and undertake such process. In addition, large constituents of the Somali people do not have any respect for warlord members that dominate the government.

Probably the AU can solve the deadlock, or major African countries such as South Africa and Nigeria, can perform the role of bringing the parties together. Nelson Mandela, which most Somalis, even ICU members, have respect for will have managed this task properly. The US does not seem able to bring peace to Somalia. Nonetheless, some unimaginable conducts took place lately. The US embassy in Nairobi and its ambassador met the leader of ICU, whom the media claims to have sought refuge in Kenya. Surprisingly, the Americans are insisting that some in the ICU leadership should be included. Some of the leadership of ICU (4-5 major players) are these days gathering in Yemen. It may after all appear that America learned its mistakes in Afghanistan and Iraq. America might therefore this time treat the Somali issue differently.

Another important aspect is that the EU, the UN and the US do not share an agenda on how, in the long term, to solve the Somali conflict. As experiences in Puntland and Somaliland show, Somalis will only enjoy viable peace when they are left alone, to combine traditional authority structure with certain form of modern state governance. Any intervention whether regional or international will only lead to more trouble and suffering for many.

---

1 In famous poem cited in Ali Jimale, Daybreak is near....., Literature, Clans and The Nation- State in Somalia, 1996

.

*Abdulkadir Osman Farah at the Centre for development and International Relations Aalborg University. He is also also employed as consultant for the municipality of Aarhus, Denmark. He is the co-founder of the Centre for Research and Integration, Aarhus, Denmark.

* Professor Mammo Muchie is Director of Research Centre on Development & International Relations at Aalborg University, Denmark

African Renaissance
Vol. 4 No.1 Quarter 1 2007
pp36-54

Penetrating Cultural Frontiers in Somalia: History of Women's Political Participation During Four Decades (1959-2000)

Abdurahman M. Abdullahi (Baadiyow)

Introduction

Somalia is a classic case of a collapsed, post-independence country in which the dissolution of its central state authority brought about a catastrophic civil war. The war began in 1991, and during its first decade, the country received enormous international attention that prompted a US-led, multi-national intervention and numerous reconciliation conferences. In such civil wars, it is women, children, and minorities who are vulnerable and they are victimized the most as a consequence. From this perspective, the war in Somalia was no exception. The patriarchal patterns of Somali society and its dominant political clans meant that women were completely excluded from the 11 failed reconciliation conferences that were held between 1991 and 2000. Ultimately, though, at the 2000 conference, a new approach was adopted. This accommodated all Somalis, including women, who gained a quota of 25 seats (10.5 per cent) from the total of 245 seats comprising the Transitional Interim Parliament.[i] Women's empowerment in the 2000 Somali Peace Conference in Djibouti has particular academic significance because Somalia is a Muslim society characterized by a patriarchal social system that is the embodiment of its Islamic and clannish structures. Moreover, this empowerment coincided with the ascendancy of the political dimensions of Islam and its clan organization, an ascendancy known to present major obstacles to the cause of women.

Two main concepts to which reference will be made here require specific definitions. These are women and politics. For the purposes of this essay, women will include those of the Somali middle class, where this class has the sociological meaning attributed to it by Max Weber. Politics in the present context is defined as the methods and processes of making decisions within groups that are identified as part of the public sphere. Such a definition of politics stems from the perspective of the "Realist" theory of "high politics", and it excludes definitions provided by "Critical" perspectives.[ii] Furthermore, political participation exclusively meant becoming members of the Transitional National Assembly (TNA) and the Transitional National Government (TNG) formed in Djibouti in 2000.

Central to the concerns of this essay are the reasons for Somali women achieving such political leverage during the period specified, for it is an achievement that challenges orientalist and anthropological images of Somali society and its women. After a short literature review, we investigate briefly the historical context of women within the cultural, religious, and political framework of Somali society. The civil war and the changing roles of genders are considered next. Finally, the enabling factors which promoted women's political empowerment at the 2000 Somali Peace Conference in Djibouti will be examined and some conclusions will be drawn.

Literature Review

It has been argued that modern Somali scholarship is dominated by orientalist and anthropological perspectives that focus on primordialism and the static nature of the traditional structures. This perspective confers a superseding influence of clan factors over all other aspects of Somali historiography.[iii] The plethora of literature produced by the proponents of this perspective has been criticized for the limitations of its scope and the flaws in its interpretations, as well as for its lack of "historical specificity in the use of key concepts".[iv] This pattern of scholarship is evident in the writings of the orientalist Richard Burton[v] and the anthropologists I. M. Lewis[vi] and Enrico Cerulli.[vii] It has been passed on to their disciples Berhard Helander[viii] and Virginia Lulling.[ix] Edwad Said and other scholars have criticized the orientalist method, ideology, and discourses. More specifically, orientalist scholars are blamed for heralding andocentric views in their analyses and promoting cultural "nomadization". At the same time, though, their analyses included the negative image described by Christine Choi Ahmed as "the myth of the Somali women as chattel, commodity, and creature with little power".[x]

By contrast, another group of Somali scholars adopt a similar critical perspective while claiming that they sustain the specificity and historicity of the interpretation of their object of analysis and the proposed "transformationist thesis". Prominent among these scholars are Lidwien Kapteijns,[xi] Ahmed Samatar,[xii] and Abdi Samatar.[xiii] For instance, besides its pastoralist dimension, Kapteijns discerns in the Somali society the existence of agrarian and city-dwellers that developed "different gender ideologies and gender roles".[xiv] On the other hand, Ahmed Samatar and Abdi Samatar agree on a more comprehensive perspective founded on analysing traditional Somali society within the triangular model comprising clan attachment (*tol*), traditional law (*heer*), and Islamic shari'a. Moreover, according to their thesis, the internal dynamics and interactions between the elements of this model are dialectically bounded by pervasive modernity. Ironically, this implies a need to examine gender relations within this multitude of parameters.[xv]

Recently, a revisionist tendency had emerged in which the two perspectives cited are criticized for accepting the constructed myths and utilizing the official narratives that contributed to the conceptualization of the old Somalia. Those who adopt this new perspective set out to demystify the conventional image of Somaliness as one constructed by idealist Somali nationalists, colonial historiographers, and post-colonial hegemonic clan interests. Moreover, they blame these latter scholars for creating a chauvinistic history focusing on pastoralists to the exclusion of the Southern agrarian population of Somalia. With this in mind, the revisionists have re-examined conventional national symbols and myths, such as racial homogeneity, linguistic unity, and common historical experiences. Prominent scholars in this group are Mohamed Mukhtar,[xvi] Ali Jumale,[xvii] Abdi Kusow,[xviii] Hassan Mahaddala,[xix] and Catherine Besteman.[xx] The major themes of their perspective can be traced in two recent works comprising collected papers: *The Invention of Somalia* edited by Jumale Ahmed and *Putting the Cart before the Horse* edited by Abdi Kusow.

With few exceptions, the common denominator among all of the above scholars is their neglect and exclusion of women as agents and active participants within their historical research. This limitation is also apparent in the major classical historical works by Ali Hersi,[xxi] Mohamed Nuh Ali,[xxii] Ahmed Ismail Samatar,[xxiii] Saadia Tauval,[xxiv] and David Laitin and Said Samatar.[xxv] Moreover, throughout the relevant academic and non-academic bibliography relating to Somalia, it is evident that Somali women are marginalized. This is the case in academia as well as in other aspects of life. Overall, the socio-economic role of Somali women is treated episodically within the works of the Somali bibliography. However, there exists a newly emerging orientation in attitudes exemplified in the book entitled *Somalia: the Untold Story* by Judith Garner and Judy El-Bushra.[xxvi]

Historical Context

The modern political development of Somalia began in the early years of the Second World War after the 1941 defeat of Italian Fascism in the Horn of Africa and the establishment of British administration in most parts of the Somali territories. British administration brought an improved political environment by abolishing the "restrictions of the Italian regime on local political associations and clubs".[xxvii] This new policy encouraged advances in the political consciousness of Somalis after many of them had participated in two wars: the Italian–Ethiopian War of 1935 and the Second World War. As a result, the Somali Youth Club (SYC), the first pan-Somali organization, was formed on 13 May 1943 in Mogadishu. From its founding membership of 13 men, this club developed into a political party in 1947 and was renamed the Somali Youth League (SYL). A comparable rise in political consciousness was appearing in the British Somali Protectorate, and this led to the establishment of the party known as the Somali National League (SNL). These two major parties, the SYL and the SNL, adopted corresponding nationalist platforms by the 1950s. At the same time, other particularistic parties were shifting towards a similar nationalist course. During this period, there existed women who were prominent in the anti-colonial movement, personified, for example, by Hawa Tako.[xxviii] However, even the most nationalistic organizations, such as the SYL, did not accept women to full membership until 1952.[xxix] This reflects the fact that women's political participation depends on a multitude of factors, the most important of which is the development of modern education.

In the Somali British Protectorate, modern schools were rare and under-funded, with attendance restricted to boys.[xxx] Girls did not participate in any formal education program until 1947 when the first elementary school for them was opened. The first secondary school in the Protectorate was established in the town of Sheikh in 1953, again with the enrolment limited to male children. And, by 1958, when the total enrolment in the schools had reached 6,209, the estimated proportion of female children in high schools remained below 20 per cent.[xxxi] At the same time, political development in the British Somali Protectorate was comparatively slow and bounded by tradition. In 1957, the first legislative council of six members was appointed by the British Governor on the basis of clan representation, and by late 1959, the legislative assembly of 30 seats was established, with most members appointed on a clan basis.[xxxii] In such a conservative society, lacking any extensive modern education, women found it difficult to gain any such universal rights as voting. Their rights were largely confined to traditional and Islamic rights.

In the Italian colony of Somalia, education was better developed than during the British administration. During World War II, Italy was defeated in 1941.[xxxiii] The subsequent administration opened 19 additional schools by 1947, with the enrolment still restricted to boys. After mandating Italy under UN Trusteeship of Somalia in 1950, socio-economic and political development took great strides to prepare the country for the independence in 1960. As Lewis observed, "by 1959 about 31,000 children and adults of both sexes were enrolled in primary schools, 246 in junior secondary schools, 336 in technical institutions, and a few hundred more in higher educational institutions".[xxxiv] On the political front, the first municipal election was held in 1954 and 16 political parties vied for 281 seats. Moreover, in 1956, the Territorial Consultative Council was transformed into a legislative assembly comprising 70 seats.[xxxv] Women were offered universal suffrage in the second municipal election of October 1958. However, no women were elected to municipal positions in that election, nor did any win seats in the subsequent parliamentary election of 1959.[xxxvi]

Women and Politics from 1960 to 1990

Post-colonial states did not break away from the established political and cultural norms of the colonial era. There was, rather, a continuation of them along with the new national symbols, slogans, and leadership. Somali politics maintained its patriarchal character, with national idealism mixed and competing with particularistic clan interests. Although women's participation in education and the civil services was increasing, their interests were not among the pressing national priorities.[xxxvii] In the post-independence period from 1960 to 1969, the two parliamentary and presidential elections that were held saw no women become members of parliament. However, the new voices of women in the urban elite were expressed in variety ways, including in the embryonic civil society organizations.[xxxviii] Moreover, a number of educated women became part of the state civil service and security forces, mostly in the lower ranks doing clerical and secretarial work. Perhaps one of the impediments to women's ascendance into the higher echelons of the bureaucracy was that few had any higher education qualifications. At the time, access to higher education was only through scholarships to foreign countries. The numbers of women who received these scholarships was small for a variety of reasons. During the first nine years of democratic Somalia, women were absent from the parliament, although one woman initiated such an attempt when she stood for a parliamentary seat in the 1969 elections.[xxxix]

In the military era from 1969 to 1990, women became more vocal and participated in the grassroots revolutionary programs of the regime. They were publicly visible, particularly in the socialist orientation centers and as members of the revolutionary security forces. They actively participated in education and took higher positions in the public service. There were women of high rank among the officers in the army and the air force, and they took up positions as general managers, ambassadors, and director generals. And, finally, women parliamentarians and vice-ministers were appointed. From 1975 to 1984, the proportion of women in public administration increased on average at a rate of 39.5 per cent annually, while in the autonomous agencies the rate was 45.3 per cent.[xl] The military regime enacted a number of laws that advantaged women, such as those ensuring equal salary for equal jobs and providing for paid maternity leave. The new family law of 1975 created enormous social and political upheaval because it contradicted the Islamic law of inheritance.[xli]

In the first years of military rule and the adoption of socialist ideology, Somalia took a new path of development. Somali script of Latin origin was adopted in 1972 to launch an ambitious educational plan. As a result, the enrolment in primary schools rose from 28,000 in 1970 to 220,000 in 1976, and to 271,000 in 1982. The number of primary schools also increased, rising from 287 in 1970 to 844 in 1975, and to 1407 in 1980. Furthermore, the number of teachers reached a peak of 3,376 in 1981.[xlii] The literacy rate reached to almost 50 per cent of the population aged 15 years and above in 1980.[xliii] However, in the difficult decade of the 1980s, education declined due to a lack of funds and political instability in the country. The literacy rate had dropped to 24 per cent by 1990.[xliv] In higher education, the Somali National University expanded and the number of students graduating annually from the 13 faculties during the period from 1985 to 1988 averaged about 924.[xlv] The proportion of female students among the graduates remained low at an estimated less than 20 per cent.[xlvi]

During the 21 years of military rule, political structures and processes were firmly in line with the espoused socialist ideology. The country was ruled in accordance with especially draconian directives from 1969 to 1976. In 1976, the Somali Socialist Revolutionary Party (SSRP) was formed and only one woman was among the 76 members of the central committees.[xlvii] To advance the interests of women, the Somali Women Democratic Organization (SWDO) was founded as a branch the SSRP in 1977. In addition, during the late 1980s, 12 women were appointed as legislators among the 176 members holding parliamentary seats. Two were appointed as vice-ministers out of the 51 ministerial positions available, although all five members of the politburo were men.[xlviii] By the 1980s, two forms of opposition were emerging, peaceful Islamic opposition and armed clan-based opposition.[xlix] Finally, the military regime disintegrated when, on 26 January 1991, armed clan-based factions overran the capital city. The Somali Republic had totally collapsed.

Women and Civil War (1990-2000)

On 28 January 1991, rather than the expected regime change, the institutions of state in Somalia collapsed. The initial joy and celebrations that met the demise of the repressive regime soon turned into dismay. The calamity that had befallen the Somalis saw a brutal civil war break out, a war that was to spread indiscriminate terror, havoc, plundering, looting, destroying, and killing across the country. In such circumstances, women, children, and minorities were the most severely affected. Moreover, the civil war caused huge displacement and the massive migration resulted in more than a million Somalis being scattered all over the world. At this critical moment, Somali civil society re-emerged to take on the role of a non-state actor that could provide essential services. Women were at the forefront of the emergent civil society organizations. What was becoming apparent was that gender roles shift dramatically during wars, the aftermath of civil wars, and under authoritarian regimes.[l] In particular, the roles of Somali women changed noticeably in all aspects of life. Aside from all sorts of victimization and exploitation concomitant with the nature of wars, many women became heads of households and breadwinners of families.[li] They cared for the old, the sick, the injured, and the orphans while most men were fighting. The role of women in the civil war expanded in the humanitarian field, the peace dialogue, and the advocacy of human rights as part of Somali civil society.

It will be argued here that three main factors had paved the way for the political empowerment of women at this particular historical juncture. These were (1) the growth of Somali civil society in the decade from 1990 to 2000; (2) the rise to prominence of moderate Islamic discourse; and (3) the failure of warlord-driven reconciliations.

Growth of modern civil society

Modern civil society in Somalia emerged as a response to the conditions of state collapse in 1991 and the outbreak of the civil war, as well as being an expression of the freedom gained after the repressive years of dictatorship. It was also stimulated by the world-wide tendency towards democratization after the end of the Cold War in the late 1990s. Moreover, the most significant threshold for modern civil society occurred during the US-led multilateral military intervention in Somalia in 1992 and the subsequent influx of hundreds of international NGOs.[lii] These NGOs required local partners to reach out to distant locations and to facilitate access to local populations, given the precarious security situation of the time. In addition, UN agencies also needed these partners to implement small-scale development projects, such as distributing seeds and repairing canals, roads, schools, and health facilities. Hence, thousands of Somali NGOs mushroomed all over the country, many of them as implementing partners. However, most of these transient organizations disbanded with the departure of the international forces and the international NGOs from Somalia in 1995. Some dedicated local NGOs remained in the areas of humanitarian operations, with their focus being primarily on education, health, peace advocacy, human rights, and professional networking. These NGOs depended mainly on locally-generated funds and advanced their organizational capacities by networking and linking to each other. According to the civil society mapping report produced by NOVIB-Somalia in 2003, among the 293 surveyed modern civil society organizations, 226 or 77 per cent were local NGOs, 33 or 11 per cent were professional associations, and 34 or 12 per cent were networks.[liii] Moreover, as well as their inclusion in specialized women's organizations, this same report noted that "women enjoy[ed] strong representation in local NGOs," with most of the surveyed organizations having "a ratio of roughly 1:4 women to men which implies that there is a gradual acceptance of women's place in the decision-making process at all levels in Somalia".[liv]

Prominence of moderate Islamic discourse

After the collapse of the Somali state in 1991, two major modern Islamic organizations gained prominence: Al-Islah and Al-Ittihad. Islah advocates an interpretation of Islam that is very similar to that of the Egyptian Muslim Brotherhood, while Al-Ittihad is considered to be in line with the neo-Salafiya Movement, a movement that has a close affinity with the Wahabi school of thought in Saudi Arabia. These organizations were founded in the late 1970s and early 1980s respectively. When the civil war broke out, they took two different approaches to dealing with the Somali debacle. Al-Ittihad's approach was more militant and involved active political engagement which motivated the armed interventions in "Lower Juba in 1991, North Eastern region in 1992 and in Gedo region in 1997-1998".[lv] Consequently, such involvement and its strict interpretation of Islam with respect to women meant that its influence dwindled. On the other hand, Islah's approach to the crisis of 1991 was non-violent and took the form of peaceful engagement. Its focus was on education and reconciliation.[lvi] In Islamic jurisprudence, the role of women in politics remains a controversial issue in the Muslim world, and the spectrum of interpretations ranges from extreme rejection to cautious participation and complete acceptance.[lvii] However, the most moderate viewpoints accept women's participation in politics in principle, with slight variations in the details. The viewpoint of Islah on women stems from its moderate interpretation of the religious texts. It has been argued that Islah openly advocates for the advancement of the rights of the women and strongly supports their social and political participation in the community affairs. The effect of this policy was so great that Somali women are playing important role in politics and social life hitherto believed the domain of men.[lviii]

With respect to the position of Al-Ittihad, it apparently concurs with the Wahabi School that relegates women to roles confined to their homes. Since Islah played an important role in the Djibouti peace conference, as many observers reported, moderate Islamic views on women eventually dominated the scene and paved the way for the success of women at the conference.[lix]

Failure of warlord-driven reconciliations

Regional and international efforts to bring lasting peace to Somalia and to recover its statehood have continued since the country's disintegration and the outbreak of civil war in 1991. Neighbouring countries such as Ethiopia, Djibouti, and Kenya have hosted most of the reconciliation conferences that have been organized. Egypt, too, has held one such reconciliation conference. Most of these conferences were supported by the UN, the IGAD, the Arab League, and the European Union. Observers report that about 11 of these reconciliation conferences occurred during the first decade of the Somali conflict, but only four were major ones. The first conference in which all faction leaders participated was held in Addis Abba in March 1993 under the sponsorship of the UN and funded by the Peace and Life Institute of Sweden.[lx] The other three major conferences were held in Kenya (1994), Ethiopia (1996), and Cairo, Egypt (1997). Participation in all these conferences was limited to the warring political factions based exclusively on clan affiliations. Critics of the conferences argued that the reasons for their continual failure were the policy of subversion and sabotage that existed between vying regional actors and the absence of civil society.[lxi] Organizers believed that Somali politics is clannish, that clans are patriarchal, and that the roles within each conference should be played by the strong men as measured by the weapons they owned and numbers of militia they commanded. After the failure of all 11 conferences, the image of the factions was tarnished to a great extent and any possibility of reconciling them significantly curtailed. As a result, they lost the support of local populations and regional sponsors.

Women and the Djibouti Peace Conference

The 2000 Somali Peace Conference in Djibouti was sponsored by the Djibouti Government. It came after ten years of catastrophic civil war that began in 1991 and espoused an innovative approach to Somali reconciliation. This turned out to be a remarkable milestone for political realism[lxii] as the conference departed from the warlord-driven process, the concept of a "building block", and the radical nationalist perspective. Consequently, hitherto underestimated factors of political division such as clans, minorities, religion, and the status of women were accounted for, recognized, and addressed within the power sharing arrangements. Djibouti President Ismail Omar Guelleh, in his capacity as the chairperson of the Intergovernmental Authority on Development (IGAD), maintained in his speech at UN headquarters on 22 September 1999 that any Somali reconciliation conference will be driven by Somali civil society. The subsequent Somali Peace Conference was held in Djibouti in two phases. Phase one was inaugurated in March 2000 with the intention of mobilizing ideas and garnering support for the conference from variety of Somali groups. The second phase was launched on 2 May 2000 and more than 2,500 Somalis participated.[lxiii] What was most difficult to resolve were the criteria for participation. After discussions and consultations concerning all the options available, the option of clan-based representation ultimately prevailed. Somalia has four major clan families, namely the Darood, the Hawiye, the Dir and Digil, and the Mirifle. There are also numerous smaller clans outside of these four major ones. What was agreed upon was a power sharing criterion of 4.5 quotas comprising four equal quotas for the major clans and one half of a quota for the alliance of small clans. Women lobbied to be considered as having separate clan status because the clans did not include them among their official delegates. They gained that privilege with the strong support of the Djibouti President Guelleh, and as a result they were able actively to participate in all facets of the conference as a sixth clan. For instance, women were well represented on the Charter Drafting Committee and the Steering Committee of the conference.[lxiv] The quota system adopted by the conference and recorded in the National Charter adopted in conference allocated 44 seats to each of the four major clans, 24 seats to the minority clan alliance, and 25 seats to women. In addition, 20 seats were designated for selected individuals as an adjustment and reconciliation gesture.

Quotas have been viewed as one of the most effective affirmative actions that can be taken to increase women's political participation. There are now 77 countries with constitutional, electoral, or political party quotas for women.[lxv] Most specifically, quota systems have significantly increased women's representation among both the elected and appointed positions that allow a contribution to political decision-making. So, the stage was set for women's empowerment at the conference, given that most of the faction leaders were absent and civil society groups became the driving force. Nevertheless, a number of pertinent questions remain to be answered. How did the women receive their quota? Who decided to offer them the quota? Who facilitated these decisions? The answers flowed from the intellectual symposium held in Djibouti in March 2000 and attended by about 60 Somali intellectuals, including a number of highly educated women. In closing this symposium, Asha Haji Ilmi, a woman and civil society activist, presented an inspiring speech in the name of Somali intellectuals. She made specific reference to the promising results that had been achieved, including that the women's group had been encouraged and were appropriately accepted as being the sixth clan attending the conference.[lxvi] This offered them the opportunity of having their representatives on the Steering Committee and Charter Drafting Committee where vital decisions of the conference were made.

Decisions about what to include in the Transitional Charter were made by the Charter Drafting Committee comprising 32 members, including five representatives of each of the six clans (four major clans, the alliance of minority clans, and the women's group) and two members from the Somali Technical Committee. The women's group was highly organized and launched an effective lobbying strategy that saw them ultimately gain 25 seats in the parliament. It is worth noting here that this outcome was achieved without either state intervention or external pressure. The conference was a purely community-based platform facilitated by the Djibouti government. Moreover, the possible influences of conservative opposition from clans, or perhaps from religious factions, had been weakened during first decade of the civil war.

Conclusion

Historical analysis has shown that although Somali women gained full political rights before independence in 1960, it nonetheless took 40 years for them to receive a constitutionally sanctioned quota in the National Assembly. The challenges and obstacles that impeded the rise of women's political participation stemmed from the political culture based on patriarchy, combined with traditional social pressures and beliefs about the historical roles of genders. Moreover, women's low educational status made it difficult for them to compete in the political sphere. This minimized their political capacity and represented one of the key challenges they faced. What the present study has shown is that there were no meaningful conservative opposition forces, legal discrimination, and/or state policies that restrained women's participation in politics. Therefore, contrary to the victimization perspective adopted by mostly Western scholars, it could be argued that Somali women enjoyed a higher status within their society than is indicated by the constructed negative images. For all intents and purposes, a rearrangement of gender roles within the new state institutions occurred gradually in its initial stages and took an exponential upsurge during the civil war.

In the final analysis, the landslide victory of Somali women in the Somali Reconciliation Conference of 2000 should be understood as a product of 40 years of cumulative struggle by local and international actors. And, it is a result that can be linked to the world-wide trends of the era. We should also bear in mind the relevance of the changed role of genders after the civil war, the proliferation of civil society ideals of mutual acceptance and participatory models, and the enhanced moderation of Islamic discourses on women. In addition, it was the decrease in the political control of the armed patriarchal factions and the decline of religious conservatism that enabled women to make such gains in their political power in 2000. The old narratives based on Islam and traditional cultures that presented impediments to women's political participation had all but disappeared by that year, at least in the Somali context. Our thesis has been that the political role of women is determined largely by the socio-economic development of the whole society around them, in particular by the level of education they can achieve and by the extent of their mobility outside the home. With all the above having been said, though, it is safe to conclude only that the improvements to the status of women in Somali society are just beginning and realized only through the affirmative action.

References

Abdi, Ali. "Education in Somalia: History, destruction, and calls for reconstruction." *Comparative Education* 34 (November 1998): 327-340. Available from www.dns tvind.dk/sis/education_in_somalia.htm. Accessed 10 November 2005.

Abdullahi, Abdurahman. "Tribalism, Nationalism and Islam: Crisis of the Political Loyalties in Somalia." MA thesis, Islamic Institute, McGill University, 1992.

Abdullahi, Abdurahman. "Tribalism and Islam: The Basics of Somaliness." In *Variations on the Theme of Somaliness, edited by* Muddle Suzanne Liluis. Turku, Finland: Centre of Continuing Education, Abo University, 2001.

Abdullahi, Abdurahman. "Non-State Actors in the Failed State of Somalia: Survey of the Civil Society Organizations in Somalia during g the Civil War." *Darasaat Ifriqiyayyah* 31 (2004): 57-87.

Abdulle, Abdulqadir Adan. Interview on 21 October 2005.

Academy of Peace Development. *The Impact of the War on the Family.* Somaliland: Hargeisa, 2002.

Affi, Laddan. "Men Drink Tea While the Women Gossip." In *Putting* the Cart before the Horse: Contested Nationalism and the Crisis of the Nation-State in Somalia, edited by Abdi Kusow. Lawrenceville: The Red Sea Press, 2004.

Ahmed, Christine Choi. "Finely Etched Chattel: The Invention of Somali Women." In *The Invention of Somalia,* edited by Jumale Ahmed. Lawrenceville: The Red Sea Press,1995.

Ahmed, Jumale. *The Invention of Somalia.* Lawrenceville: The Red Sea Press, 1995.

Ali Hersi. *The Arab Factor in Somali Society: the Origins and Development of Arab Enterprise and Cultural Influence in the Somali Peninsula.* Los Angeles: University of California, Los Angeles, 1977.

Beckman, Peter R., and Francine D'Amico, eds. *Women in World Politics: An Introduction.* Greenwood Press,1995.

Besteman, Catherine. *Unravelling Somalia: Race, Violence, and the Legacy of Slavery.* University of Pennsylvania Press, 1999.

Bryden, Matt. "No Quick Fixes: Coming into Terms with Terrorism, Islam, and Statelessness in Somalia." *Journal of Conflict Studies* 22 (fall 2003).

Brons, Maria. "The Civil War in Somalia: Its Genesis and Dynamics." *Current African Issues* 11 (1991).

Brons, Maria. *Society, Security, Sovereignty and the State in Somali: from Statelessness to Statelessness?.* Nederland: International Books, 2001.

Gardner, Judith, and Judy Al-Bushra. *Somalia: The Untold Story, the War Though the Eyes of Somali Women.* London: Pluto Press, 2004.

Hassan, Nurta Hagi. Interview on 25 October, 2005.

Horn of African Center for Information and Studies. "Islah in Somalia: Views and Policies on Major Contemporary Issues." Unpublished paper, Mogadishu, Somalia, 2003.

Ilmi, Asha Haji. Interview on 25 October 2005.

Kapteijns, Lidwien. "Women and Crisis of Communal Identity: The Cultural Construction of Gender in Somali History." In *The Somali Challenge: From Catastrophe to Renewal?,* edited by Samatar Ahmed. Boulder: Lynne Reinner Publishers, 1994.

Kapteijns, Lidwien, and Maryan Omar Ali. *Women's voices in a man's world: women and the pastoral tradition in Northern Somali Orature, c.1899-1980.* Portsmouth, NH: Heinemann, 1999.

Kusow, Abdi, ed. *Putting the Cart before the Horse: Contested Nationalism and the Crisis of the Nation-State in Somalia.* Lawrenceville: The Red Sea Press, 2004.

Laitin, David D., and Said Samatar. *Somalia: Nation in Search of a State.* Boulder: Westview Press, 1987.

Le Sage, Andre. "Al-Islah in Somalia: An analysis of modernist political Islam." Unpublished paper, 2004.

Lewis, I. M. *A Modern History of Somalia: Nation and State in the Horn of Africa.* London: Longmans, 1980.

Marshal, Ronald. "Islamic Political Dynamics in the Somali Civil War".

Paper presented at the conference on "Islam in Africa: A Global, Cultural and Historical Perspective." Institute of Global Cultural Studies, Birmingham University, 2001.

Ministry of National Planning. *Statistical Data of Somalia in Figures*. Mogadishu: National Printing Agency, 1988. Available from www.genie.og/genie-crises-links/peer/pdf/SIFEDU3.pdf. Accessed 10 November 2005. _

Mukhtar, Mohamed. "Islam in Somali History: Fact and Fiction." In *The Invention of Somalia*, edited by Jumale Ahmed. Lawrenceville: The Red Sea Press, 1995.

NOVIB-Somalia. "Arab Donor Policies and Practices on Education in Somalia/Somaliland." September 2004. Available from http://www.somali-civilsociety.org/downloads/NOVIB-WAMY-FINAL.pdf. Accessed 10 November 2005.

NOVIB-Somalia. "Mapping Somali Civil Society." Nairobi: Kenya, 2003. Available from http://www.somali-civilsociety.org/strength/phase1_Mapping%20somalicivilsociety.asp. Accessed 10 November 2005.

Nuh Mohamed. *History in the Horn of Africa, 1000 BC to 1500 AD*. Los Angeles: University of California, Los Angeles, 1985.

Pastaloza, Luigi. *The Somali Revolution. Bari:* Edition Afrique Asie Amerique Latine, 1973.

Progress of the World's Women: Most positive change seen in women's political participation." Available from www. portal.unesco.org. Accessed 10 November 2005.

Rage, Abdurahman O. "Somali NGOs: a product of crisis." In *Mending Rips in the Sky* edited by Adam and Ford. Asamara: Red Sea Press, 1997.

Rodriguez Bello, Carolina. "Women and Political Participation." November 2003. Available from http://www.whrnet.org/docs/issue-women-politics.html. Accessed 10 November 2005.

Samatar, Abdi Ismail. "Destruction of State and Society in Somalia: Beyond the Tribal Convention." *Journal of Modern African Studies* 30 (1992): 625-647.

Samatar, Ahmed. *Socialist Somalia: Rhetoric and Reality*. London: Zed Press, 1988.

Samatar, Ahmed. "The Curse of Allah: Civic Disembowelment and the Collapse of the State in Somalia." In *The Somali Challenge: From Catastrophe to Renewal?*, edited by Ahmed Samatar. Boulder: Lynne Reinner Publishers, 1994.

Samatar, Ahmed, ed. *The Somali Challenge: From Catastrophe to Renewal?* Boulder: Lynne Reinner Publishers, 1994.

Tahir, Mahmood. *Personal Law in Islamic Countries*
. New Delhi: Academy of Law and Religion, 1987.

Tauval, Saadia. *Somali Nationalism*. Cambridge: Cambridge University

Press, 1963.

Notes

2. This percentage was the highest level of women's representation within Arab parliaments. By comparison, Syria had 8.4%, Sudan 8.2%, Algeria 7%, Tunisia 6.8%, and rest of Arab World less than 3% (see "Progress of Arab women", a report produced by UNIFEM in the year 2004, available from www.arabwomenconnect.org, accessed 10 November 2005). In comparison with women parliamentarians in Africa as a whole, 13 countries have a larger percentage, including South Africa and Mozambique with 30 %, and Rwanda and Uganda with 25.7% and 24.7% respectively (see "Progress of the World's Women: Most positive change seen in women's political participation", available from www. portal.unesco.org, accessed 10 November 2005).

3. Peter R. Beckman and Francine D'Amico eds, *Women in World Politics: An Introduction* (Greenwood Press, 1995), 1-10.

4. Lidwien Kapteijns, "Women and Crisis of Communal Identity: The Cultural Construction of Gender in Somali History," in *The Somali Challenge: From Catastrophe to Renewal?* ed. Ahmed Samatar (Colorado: Lynne Reinner Publishers, 1994), 212. Also, Abdi I. Samatar, "Destruction of State and Society in Somalia: Beyond the Tribal Convention," *The Journal of the Modern African Studies* 30 (1992): 625-641.

5. Ibid., 629.

6. Richard Burton, *First Footstep in East Africa* (New York: Paeger, 1966).

7. Professor of Anthropology, London School of Economics. He wrote his PhD thesis on Somalia in the 1950s and since then he has written extensively on Somalia. His numerous works are considered indispensable references on Somalia.

8. Italian ethnologist, employed by the Italian Administration in Somalia. He wrote extensively on Somali ethnology.

9. Swedish anthropologist who wrote his PhD thesis on Somalia. Currently works for Uppsala University, Sweden.

10. An Anthropologist who wrote her PhD on the Somali Sultanate of Geledi.

11. Christine Choi Ahmed, "Finely Etched Chattel: The Invention of Somali Women," in *The Invention of Somalia,* ed. Jumale Ahmed (Lawrenceville: The Red Sea Press, 1995), 159.

12. Lidwien Kapteijns is Associate Professor of History at Wellesley College, Massachusetts and has written many works on Somali women.

13. Ahmed I. Samatar is Dean of International Studies at McAlester College, St. Paul, Minnesota and has written a number of works on Somalia.

14. Abdi Samatar is Professor of Geography and Global Studies at the

University of Minnesota, USA.

15. Kapteijns, 214.

16. Ahmed Samatar, "The Curse of Allah: Civic Disembowelment and the Collapse of the State in Somalia," in *The Somali Challenge: From Catastrophe to Renewal?*, ed. Ahmed Samatar (Colorado: Lynne Rienner Publishers, 1994), 111. See also Abdi Samatar, "Destruction of State and Society in Somalia", 630.

17. Professor of African History at Savannah State University. He received his PhD from Al-Azhar University, Cairo, Egypt, and has written extensively on the revisionist historiography of Somalia.

18. Associate Professor, Department of Comparative Literature, Queens Collage, New York.

19. Associate Professor, Department of Sociology and Anthropology, Oakland University, Rochester, Michigan.

20. Associate Professor of Political Science, Southern University, USA.

21. Associate Professor of Anthropology at Colby College, USA.

22. Ali Hersi, *The Arab Factor in Somali Society: the Origins and Development of Arab Enterprise and Cultural Influence in the Somali Peninsula* (Los Angeles: University of California, Los Angeles, 1977).

23. Mohamed Nuh, *History in the Horn of Africa, 1000 BC to 1500 AD* (Los Angeles: University of California, Los Angeles, 1985).

24. Ahmed Samatar, *Socialist Somalia: Rhetoric and Reality* (London: Zed Press, 1988).

25. Sadia Tauval, *Somali Nationalism* (Cambridge: Cambridge University Press, 1963).

26. David Laitin and Said Samatar, *Somalia: Nation in Search of a State* (Boulder: Westview Press, 1987).

27. Judith Garner and Judy El-Bishra, *Somalia, the Untold Story: the War Though the Eyes of Somali Women* (London: Pluto Press, 2004).

28. Lewis, I. M., *Modern History of Somalia: Nation and State in the Horn of Africa* (Colorado, Boulder: University Press, 2002), 121.

29. Hawa Tako is recognized as one of the great Somali heroes during anti-colonial struggle. The Military Regime built a monument to honour her in Mogadishu.

30. Laddan Affi, "Men Drink Tea While the Women Gossip," in *Putting the Cart before the Horse: Contested Nationalism and the Crisis of the Nation-State in Somalia*, ed. Abdi Kusow (Asmara: The Red Sea Press, 2004), 98.

31. From 1945 to 1948, numbers of elementary schools rose from seven to eight, with the enrolment increasing from 400 to 433 boys.

32. Abdurahman Abdullahi, "Tribalism, Nationalism and Islam: Crisis of the Political Loyalties in Somalia", (MA Thesis, McGill University, 1992), 64.

i Lewis, *Modern History of Somalia*, 152.

34. The number of Somalis in elementary schools rose from 1,390 to 1,777

between 1930 and 1939, and they were enrolled in 12 elementary schools run by the Catholic missions (see Tauval, *Somali Nationalism,* 73 and Abdullahi, "Tribalism, Nationalism and Islam," 64.

35. Lewis, *Modern History of Somalia,* 140-141.

36. Membership of the assembly was allocated in accordance with a quota system, with 60 seats designated for the Somalis and 10 seats for minorities, such as Italians, Yemenis, and Indo-Pakistanis.

37. The early political ambition of women was expressed when a delegation of women SYL members led by Khadija Muse Matan met with President Adan Abdulle Osman in 1959 and demanded that they be included in the list of the candidates of the SYL party. The President cautioned them that this was a premature step in the Somali political process (interview with Abdulqadir Adan Abdulle, son of the first President of Somalia, 21 October 2005).

38. In May 1961, the law of universal suffrage was passed in the parliament (Lewis, *Modern History of Somalia,* 178.

39. Abdurahman Abdullahi, "Non-state Actors in the Failed State of Somalia: Survey of the Civil Society Organizations in Somalia during the Civil War," *Darasaat Ifriqiyyah* 31 (2004): 57-87.

40. This lady vied for the parliamentary seat in the El-Bur District in 1969. Her name was Hawa Yarey.

41. Maria Brons, *Society, Security Sovereignty and the State in Somalia* (Nederland: International Books, 2001), 199.

42. Mahmood Tahir, *Personal Law in Islamic Countries* (New Delhi: Academy of Law and Religion, 1987), 253-262. Also see Article 55 of the Somali Workers Stature and Labour Code of 1972.

43. The ambitious literacy campaign was launched all over Somalia. For detailed statistics, see Luigi Pastaloza, *The Somali Revolution* (Bari: Edition Afrique Asie Amerique Latine, 1973), 268.

44. NOVIB-Somalia, "Arab Donor Policies and Practices on Education in Somalia/Somaliland," available from http://www.somali-civilsociety.org/downloads/NOVIB-WAMY-FINAL.pdf (September 2004), accessed 10 November 2005.

45. *Ali Abdi, "Education in Somalia: History, destruction, and calls for reconstruction," Comparative Education 34, November 1998, 327-340, available from www.dns-tvind.dk/sis/education_in_somalia.htm, accessed 10 November 2005.*

46. Graduates in 1985, 1986, 1987, and 1988 were 876, 835, 1370, and 635 respectively (see statistical data of Somalia in figures, Ministry of National Planning, Mogadishu, 1988, 16, available from www.genie.og/genie-crises-links/peer/pdf/SIFEDU3.pdf, accessed 10 November 2005). _

47. Interview with Nurta H. Hassan on 25 October 2005.

48. Gardner and Al-Bushra, *Somalia: the Untold Story,* 177. The only woman in the central committee of the SSRP was Fatuma Omar Hashi.

49. Ibid. and telephone interview with Nurta Hagi Hassan (Toronto,

Canada) on 25 October 2005..

50. The Islamic oppositions were mainly Al-Ittihad, Al-Islah, and others, while the main armed factions were the Somali Salvation Democratic Front (SSDF) (1978), the Somali National Movement (SNM) (1981), the United Somali Congress (USC) (1989), and the Somali Patriotic Movement (SPM) (1988).

51. Osseina Alidou and Meredeth Turshen, "Africa: Women in the Aftermath of Civil war", *Race & Class,* 2000:41(4):81-92.

52. A UNICEF survey conducted early in 1996 in Somaliland found that 40 per cent of all households in randomly selected clusters were female-headed (see Academy of Peace of Development, *The Impact of the War on the Family* (Somaliland: Hargeisa, 2002).

53. On the emergence of the local NGOs refer to Abdurahman Rage, "Somali NGOs: a product of crisis," in *Mending Rips in the Sky,* eds. Adam Hussien & Richard Ford (Asmara: Red Sea Press, 1997).

54. A Report of NOVIB-Somalia, *Mapping Somali Civil Society,* (Nairobi, Kenya, 2003) 22, available from http://www.somali-civilsociety.org/strength/phase1_Mapping%20somalicivilsociety.asp, accessed 10 November 2005.

55. Ibid..

56. Abdurahman Abdullahi, "Tribalism and Islam: Variations on the Basics of Somaliness" in *Variations on the theme of Somaliness. Proceedings of the EASS/SSIA International Congress of Somali Studies,* ed. Muddle Suzanne Lilius (Turku, Finland: Center for Continuing Education, Abo University, 1998), 236.

57. Ibid..

58. The prominence of moderation in Somalia was apparent in the Borama Conference of 1993 in which clan elders participated. Women demanded full participation and clan elders accepted this conditionally if Sharia law permitted it. However, Islamic scholars issued a fatwa against allowing women to participate fully in the conference. See Gardner and Al-Bushra, *Somalia the Untold Story,* 205.

59. "Islah in Somalia: Views and Policies on Major Contemporary Issues," unpublished paper produced by the Horn of African Center for Information and Studies, Mogadishu, Somalia, 2003, 20.

60. Ronald Marshal, "Islamic Political dynamics in the Somali civil war", paper presented at the conference on "Islam in Africa: A global, cultural and Historical Perspective", Institute of Global Cultural Studies, Birmingham University, April 19-21, 2001, 5. See also Matt Bryden, "No Quick Fixes: Coming to Terms with Terrorism, Islam, and Statelessness in Somalia", *Journal of Conflict Studies* 22 (2003) and Andre le Sage, "Al-Islah in Somalia: An analysis of modernist political Islam", unpublished paper, 2004.

61. At the conclusion of this conference, it was agreed that at the next conference held, the participants would be representatives of the 18 regions of

Somalia, each region sending four delegates, including one woman. However, the next conference failed and the participation by women did not eventuate.

62. Abdullahi, "Tribalism and Islam", 237.

63. Before the Djibouti conference, reconciliation conferences were attended only by political faction leaders.

64. Official delegates numbered 810, consisting of four clan delegations of 180, each including 20 women, and 90 minority clan alliance representatives, including ten women. Among the 810 delegates, women gained 90 delegate places, or about 9 per cent of the delegates. In addition to this, more than 1,500 observers were allowed to attend the conference.

65. Mrs Asha Haji Ilmi was among the members of five Somali Steering Committees of the conference. And, among the 32 members in the Charter Drafting Committees, five were highly qualified women.

66. Carolina Rodriguez Bello, "Women and Political Participation" (November 2003), available from http://www.whrnet.org/docs/issue-women-politics.html, accessed 10 November 2005.

67. Interview with Asha Haji Ilmi on 25 October 2005. Asha Haji Ilmi was selected to represent women on the Steering Committee of the Somali Reconciliation Conference and currently she is a leading womeactivist and a member of parliament.

African Performance Review

APR

Annual Subscription Rates

Companies/orgs./institutions: £180
(including access to the online editions)

Individuals: online and Print: £60
Individuals: Online only: £30

Retail sales:
Individuals (print)   £20 (+ P&P)
Online   £10 per issue

To contribute, contact the journal's editor;

The Editor, (Dr Osita Okagbue)
Department of Drama, Goldsmiths, University of London,
SE14 6NW United Kingdom. Tel: +44 (0)207 919-7581.
Email: AfTA@gold.ac.uk.

Subscription enquiries,

please contact: sales@adonis-abbey.com

Adonis & Abbey Publishers Ltd
P.O. Box 43418,
London
SE11 4XZ
United Kingdom
Tel.: +44 (0) 2077938893

African Renaissance
Vol. 4 No.1 Quarter 1 2007
pp56-64

Re-imagining the Horn

Daniel E. Alemu

Introduction

Africa's history has been misread and misinterpreted both by European scholars and miseducated African scholars alike, who both reflect unto this history through Eurocentric convictions. For many decades, major African civilizations such as Egypt, Great Zimbabwe and Axum were all uncritically perceived to be the product of alien agents rather than indigenous African peoples. The Ethiopian case in particular, provides a unique opportunity to dwell unto this thesis. Ethiopian historiography largely rested on the hypothesis that the Ethiopian state and civilization were built by immigrants from South Arabia who colonized Ethiopia in the first millennium B.C.1 From here the invaluable contribution of alien factors in the making of ancient Ethiopian history was asserted and a genealogical link between these immigrants and the northern and central highlanders (the Abyssinians) was made. The latter point, the uncritical assertion of the belonging of the peoples of Ethiopia inhabiting the northern and central highlands to alien origins, held more serious and far-reaching ramifications. The seriousness of these on contemporary Ethiopian politics unraveled itself only in the past few decades, when arguments for 'indigenousness' were exploited to justify claims for a colonial occupation and reinforce the colonial thesis according to which the people of the northern highlands colonized those of the south, in particular the Oromo. In the view of Oromo nationalists, the pretext for secessionism or even 'independence' is in the argument that this history proves that the respective peoples whom the 'alien' northern highlanders (the Amhara and Tigreans) ruled were colonized peoples under an alien domination.

This account alerts to the fragility of history in face of ethno-nationalistic claims made by African elites, who seek to reconstruct historical narratives that serve their present political purposes. It also reveals processes of complex identity formation like that of the Oromo, whose dispersion over a vast area of land and cultural adaptability in the areas they settled in, deem the definition of "any conception of 'being

Oromo' which can be made to serve a coherent political purpose" nearly impossible.2 Yet it remains a fact that the insistence of the elite to imagine a uniform ethnic community over a given time and place constitutes a serious challenge to traditional historical narratives that are not immune in their turn to myths and fantasies.

In this paper I will discuss how constructions and reconstructions of Ethiopian historiography are put to serve political agendas through elitist inventions of 'ethnic' identities and communities. The political challenges that Ethiopia faced in her recent history require a closer examination as to the relevance of this historiography to contemporary politics and its potential role in future political development in the country. This paper seeks to uncover the political forces that are at play in constructing and reconstructing a country's past. It will be argued that the current entanglement and surge of ethnic identities is partly traceable to a Eurocentric reading of Ethiopian history. Furthermore, it seeks to highlight and reemphasize the need for an alternative writing of Ethiopian history that will settle with the larger need for a political renaissance in the region.

Revising Ethiopian Historiography

Historians have for long entertained the idea that "the ultimate origins of the Ethiopian state lie in the remote past, when Sabaean settlements were established in northern Ethiopia..."3 According to this "Orientalist Semiticist paradigm" in the words of Tibebu,4 a long tradition tracing back the Ethiopian civilization in particular Axum to South Arabian alien immigrants has been maintained. These immigrants, it was believed, colonized Ethiopia throughout the first millennium B.C. and built the Axumite civilization. This tradition began with the German orientalist Ludolf5 and was expounded later uncritically by other notorious Ethiopianists in particular Carlo Conti Rossini, Edward Ullendorff and most tragically Tadesse Tamrat.6 The underlying reasoning for this tradition was the conviction that "black people are incapable of great achievements,"7 which buttressed the way western scholars perceived the "Ethiopian Anomaly" to use Kebede's designation.8 From here, "since the appearance of an advanced civilization in Ethiopia is about to refute the Eurocentric construction of the world," observes Kebede "this threat to Eurocentrism will be removed only if what native peoples were able to achieve in Ethiopia is ascribed to non-African immigrants."9 In that spirit, the 'Orientalist Semiticist paradigm' that was propagated served this purpose well through negating the Axumites' and the Habashats' indigenousness. This sweeping negation of the indigenousness of the agents of civilization was also evident in the case of the Empire of Great Zimbabwe, where an externalization of the identity of these agents was maintained for many decades. It is noteworthy in the case of Ethiopia that even though no archeological evidence seems to have ever existed to support the hypothesis regarding the alien origins of the Axumites and the Habashats, alternatively making it more plausible to argue for the indigenousness of both,10 it was only in the past two decades though that any serious attempt was made to challenge this long tradition.

In 1988 two scholars vehemently challenged this tradition.11 They cautiously questioned this mainstream view and after reviewing some philological and historical evidence concluded that "no single evidence for direct South Arabian rule in Ethiopia has been demonstrated..."12 but that a civilizational and cultural interaction that was mutual and reciprocal in nature might have existed. They further noted that by the same token, one could exaggerate the fact that Ethiopia not only dominated and colonized South Arabia in certain historical periods but also exerted most considerable influence in the shaping of its civilization rather than the opposite.13 More recently, Ayele Bekerie mounted a more serious challenge through masterfully demonstrating the indigenousness of the Ethiopian writing system, long thought to have originated in South Arabia and thus refuted the arguments for a South Arabian origin of the Ethiopic script.14 Nevertheless, none of these works attempted to capture or assess the inherent and far-reaching political ramifications this Eurocentric view of Ethiopian history could have had on contemporary Ethiopian politics.

In recent years, few seminal works revealed that the more recent reconstructions of Ethiopian historiography drew also from the 'Orientalist Semiticist paradigm.' One notable work is that of Triulzi, who showed that in the more recent historiography of Ethiopia, where the country's past was contested and reconstructed,15 political convictions underlined the writing of historical narratives whose main purpose was to forge distinct ethno-national identities. In that setting, the question of 'alienness' and 'indigenousness' becomes a central bone of contention as the Oromo case proves.16 This latter point was elaborated more clearly by Messay Kebede who drew a clear line between this Eurocentric reading of ancient Ethiopian history and Ethiopia's current deconstruction by few historians into an agglomeration of ethnic-national communities brought together coercively by an alien 'Abyssinian' colonization.17 According to Kebede, the notion of 'Semitization' in ancient Ethiopian history, which invokes an alien domination of an indigenous population, has unmistakable implications for the way the contemporary modern state of Ethiopia is perceived and for the emergence of a colonial discourse among its peoples. In its essence, the colonial thesis suffers from numerous theoretical limitations that deem its serious consideration almost impossible. Even though discussing this colonial thesis in depth is beyond the scope of this paper, however, for our purposes it remains important to illustrate that even the "historiography of dissent"18 of the Oromo that was supposedly constructed to counter the historiography of domination entertained by the 'Abyssinians' shares exactly the same basic Eurocentric assumption of the Abyssinians' alien origins, however reconstructed in a more serviceable manner to the Oromo cause.

The Colonial Thesis

One of the most salient features defining the 'colonial situation' was identified by Balandier as "the domination imposed by a foreign minority...on an indigenous population constituting a numerical majority but inferior to the dominant group from a material point of view."19 This characteristic, in particular its two opposite components of 'alienness' and 'indigenousness' are usually evoked by some nationalistic historians so as to underpin their claims for an Ethiopian colonialism. In the case of Eritrea, the 'unique' historical experience under Italian colonialism and the violation of the late Emperor Haile-Selassie of the United Nations Resolution recognizing Eritrea as a federated state with Ethiopia and not a mere province, provided Eritrean nationalists the pretext to argue for a distinct Eritrean national identity and a colonial case. This national identity rested on the assumption that Eritreans constituted an indigenous people with their own peculiar history and identity, on which Ethiopianess was imposed upon against their will. It follows that the Eritrean people were a 'colonized' people under Ethiopian domination making the demand for independence the more plausible.20 More notable and relevant to our discussion is the Oromo case; Oromo nationalists argued that European tutelage of Ethiopia helped it arise as a "dependent colonialist power."21 This tutelage, it was argued, enabled the "outsiders"22 in the words of Holocomb and Ibssa to colonize the Oromo and the remainder of the Southern peoples.

Both accounts, the Eritrean but in particular that of the Oromo, rest exclusively on a very similar Eurocentric reconstruction of Ethiopian historiography as the one they set out originally to challenge, where the indigenousness of one people is asserted against the alienness of another. Triulzi provides that the 'historiography of dissent' that was produced by Oromo nationalists to counter mainstream Ethiopian historiography, exploited the indigenousness question to show that rather than the Oromo being the 'alien invaders,' the Amhara and the Tigreans, which Jalata accounts for as being "the children of Arab immigrants and Africans"23 were the 'alien colonizers' that colonized the indigenous populations of Ethiopia, including the Oromo. This insistence by Oromo nationalists on "the Arab or Semitic element in the making of the 'Abyssinians', and the indigenous Oromo ancestors" as put by Triulzi, is exploited "to deny the alleged 'Arab' descendants the right to declare themselves part of the same 'belonging'...."24 There is no denying that this reconstruction of history fits well with the politics of identity formation dominating the Ethiopian current national discourse and exploited to deconstruct and reconstruct imagined ethnic communities. In studying the effects of the reconstruction of history both in the Greek and Hawaiian cases Friedman recalls, "making

59

history is a way of producing identity insofar as it produces a relation between that which supposedly occurred in the past and the present state of affairs."25 Since the present social reality configures the way the past is viewed, thus reducing the past only to an extension of the present, it follows, according to Friedman, that modern historiography rather than be considered as a genuine documentation of a "historical process," which Friedman defines as "the continuous and transformational process of social reproduction over time", is reduced to a process of mythmaking.26 In the Ethiopian case, the rewriting of historical narratives on the basis of newly imagined ethnic communities entailed the creation of an exclusionary group identity confined to "cultural and linguistic bounds", and simultaneously subjecting this historical revisionism to "ideological and political overtones."27 The outcome is a mythical romanticization of the past along nationalistic-ethnic lines, rather than a historical enquiry into the past to unearth past injustices and advance our knowledge of Ethiopia's burdened history, in a way that will allow us to ameliorate these injustices satisfactorily.

If Friedman's assertion that "constructing the past is an act of self-identification"28 is accepted, then this begs the question as to how can one imagine the endurance of the idea of Ethiopia, when rewritten historical narratives and reconstructed ethnic identities are found to be exclusionary and opposed in nature, furthermore are found only to reflect sectarian and narrow based interests rather than nation-based interests? A reply to this question is perhaps provided by Clapham,29 who argues that embarking upon such a project necessitates a contemplation that transcends the confines of present-day Ethiopia to embrace the larger region, the Horn of Africa, where historically communities have intermingled, historical narratives were reconstructed and identities redefined constantly to meet political and economic needs of the time.

Re-imagining the Horn

The 'Great Tradition' in Ethiopian historiography in the words of Clapham, has generated a country "overburdened by its past"30 in which competing historical narratives came to serve political agendas of constructing opposed ethnic identities. The elitist reconstruction of history constitutes no historical anomaly neither in Ethiopia, the larger Horn nor anywhere else for that matter. Elites have always tried to appropriate 'history' in processes of forging and inventing a nationalistic consciousness and an ethnic identity. On the latter point, Abner Cohen reveals how the Hausa in Ibadan adopted a distinctive social formation, while totally integrating and assimilating within the Yoruba in other parts of colonial Nigeria. This new social formation led eventually to the creation of a distinct ethnic identity. Cohen explains this phenomenon by applying an instrumentalist approach to ethnicity, through which interest groups tend to reconstruct a distinct ethnic identity so as to efficiently compete with other groups for power.31 Needless to say, these interest groups are usually comprised of ambitious elites with opportunistic ends, whose hunger for power leads them to exploit any element from their constructed cultural repertoire so as to redraw boundaries between groups and sharpen differences to achieve their ends. This has been largely the case in Ethiopia, whether it was the Great Tradition and its accompanying national Solomonic ethos or the counter-traditions that were constructed by dissentient nationalistic historians. In that sense, the Amhara, Tigreans, Oromo, Somali, Eritreans, Afar and others have all tried through their constructed historical narratives to claim the lion's share of the history of Greater Ethiopia or the Greater Horn. Yet there is no doubt that while the Great Tradition in Ethiopian historiography was constructed in a more inclusive and dynamic manner in the sense that ethnicity came to play little role and instead imposition of certain cultural features was legitimized at the expense of others, the new historiographies however were constructed in a very exclusionary manner, appealing only to specific segments of the Ethiopian society, and some even assuming an essentialist biological ethnicist core. From here the quest for a common denominator becomes the more urgent and at the same time the more challenging.

Since the project of writing Ethiopia's history was largely undertaken from a state-centered perspective revolving around the history associated solely with the Ethiopian state as Clapham accurately contends, all other alternative historical narratives that belonged to acephalous communities that did not develop state institutions were subordinated.32 This 'Great tradition' in the writing of Ethiopian history has reflected unto the past in retrospective. It generated an urgent need to appropriate the past into present needs. The past is merely considered for its extended function and utility to the present. This leads to an ahistorical nature of Ethiopian history in which it paradoxically becomes unaccountable to the past but to the present. It is this teleological reading of Ethiopian history that Clapham opposes. Alternatively however, Clapham suggests that any new historiography of Ethiopia should be written only as part of a larger project, that of the Horn. Clapham identifies geography as playing the pivotal role in the future historiography of the Horn. Geography sets the spatial and temporal confines in which history, economics, society and identity are all constructed and delineated. In that sense, it serves as the strongest and most basic denominator that ties the peoples of the region into one collectivity that shares political, economic and social interests.

This project becomes the more important when one considers how geography too was exploited imaginatively by the proponents of the Orientalist Semiticist paradigm to redraw the spatial boundaries of Ethiopia so as to be incorporated in the Middle East.33 In the Great Tradition of Ethiopian historiography, one finds similarly that it led to the deafricanization of Ethiopia and the relocation of her origins to civilizations on the other side of the red sea.34 So given that a regional history of the Horn to which all its peoples can easily identify with and that does not favor one group's historiography over another is constructed, how can such a historical narrative correspond to wider political processes? In other words, how can this self-identification with a broadly conceived historiography be reconciled with the process of creating political identities? An answer to this question necessitates first a departure from the "intellectual log-jam" that essentially perceives the nation-state as the only legitimate form of political organization in Africa.35 The Horn of Africa as a common cultural, economic, social and political area defies the logic of nation-states. It becomes more plausible to imagine a federation of states put together by the prerequisites of a viable and interdependent regional economy and political reality. Yet here too the Great Tradition exerts an intolerable burden on any attempt to deconstruct and reconstruct the Ethiopian nation-state into a member state of a larger federation. Therefore, any political renaissance in Ethiopia in particular and the Horn in general necessitates first the deconstruction of the Great Tradition in Ethiopian historiography to components that will be more favorable to the viable future political settlement.

Conclusion

The origins of the contentious nature of current Ethiopian historiography can be traced back to early Eurocentric formulations of its founding myths. These formulations lent validity to ethnicist historical narratives aiming at creating exclusionary group identities. It was suggested in this article that indeed a rewriting of a more inclusive and comprehensive historiography in lines with Clapham's proposition is necessary. Nevertheless, this historiography should be aimed at the eventual creation of a common political identity that transcends narrow group interests and thus can be shared by all the peoples of the Horn, which might indeed necessitate the redrawing and elimination altogether of fictitious internal boundaries. The failure to create such an identity, which all the peoples of the Horn can intelligibly internalize and adopt, might undermine the seriousness of such project and reduce it to yet another elitist invention that will be reconstructed by a competing historical narrative.

References

1 T. Tamrat, (1972) *Church and State in Ethiopia: 1270-1527*, (Oxford: Clarendon Press).

2 C. Clapham, (1988) *Transformation and Continuity in Revolutionary Ethiopia*, (Cambridge: Cambridge University Press). p. 26

3 Tamrat, *Church and State in Ethiopia*, p. 5

4 T. Tibebu, (1995) *The Making of Modern Ethiopia: 1896-1974*, (The Red Sea Press). p. xvii

5 A. Bekerie, (1997) *Ethiopic, An African Writing System: Its History and Principles*, (The Red Sea Press). p. 32

6 For a review of the evolution of this paradigm and its main proponents see A. Bekerie, *Ethiopic*, Ch. 1

7 M. Kebede, (2003) "Eurocentrism and Ethiopian Historiography: Deconstructing Semitization", *International Journal of Ethiopian Studies*, Vol. 1, No. 1 (Tsehai Publishers). p. 4

8 *ibid*

9 *ibid*, p. 6

10 R. Fattovich, (2000) "Aksum and the Habashat: State and Ethnicity in Ancient Northern Ethiopia and Eritrea", *Working Papers in African Studies*, No. 228, (Boston University: African Studies Center). p. 23

11 E. Isaac and C. Felder, (1988) 'Reflections on the Origins of the Ethiopian Civilization', in T. Beyene (ed.), *Proceedings of the Eighth International Conference of Ethiopian Studies, Vol. 1*, (Addis Ababa: Institute of Ethiopian Studies).

12 *ibid*, p. 80

13 *ibid*, p. 81

14 Bekerie, *Ethiopic*

15 A. Triulzi, (2002) 'Battling with the Past: New Frameworks for Ethiopian Historiography', in W. James, D. Donham, E. Kurimoto and A. Triulzi (eds.), *Remapping Ethiopia: Socialism & After*, (Oxford: James Currey). p. 276

16 *ibid*, p. 286

17 Kebede, *Eurocentrism and Ethiopian Historiography*, p. 11

18 Triulzi, *Battling with the Past*, p. 286

19 G. Balandier, (1951) 1966 'The Colonial Situation: A Theoretical Approach', in I. Wallerstein (ed.), *Social Change: The Colonial Situation*, (New York: J. Wiley). p. 54

20 B. Habte Selassie, (1980) 'From British Rule to Federation and Annexation', in B. Davidson, L. Cliffe and B. Habte Selassie (eds.), *Behind the War in Eritrea*, (Spokesman, Russell Press: Nottingham). p. 45

21 A. Jalata, (1993) *Oromia and Ethiopia: State Formation and Ethnonational Conflict, 1868-1992*, (Boulder: Lynne Rienner Publishers). p. 8

22 B. Holcomb and S. Ibssa, (1990) *The Invention of Ethiopia*, (New Jersey: The Red Sea Press). p. 12

23 Jalata, *Oromia and Ethiopia*, p. 6

24 Trulzi, *Battling with the Past*, p. 286

25 J. Friedman, (1992) "The Past in the Future: History and the Politics of Identity", *American Anthropologist*, New Series, Vol. 94, No. 4. p. 837

26 *ibid*, p. 853

27 Triulzi, *Battling with the Past*, p. 280

28 Friedman, *The Past in the Future*, p. 856

29 C. Clapham, (2002) 'Rewriting Ethiopian History', in Centre Français d'Etudes Ethiopiennes (ed.), *Annales d'Ethiopie* (Editions Table Ronde, Addis Ababa).

30 Triulzi, *Battling with the Past*, p. 280

31 A. Cohen, (1969) *Custom and Politics in Urban Africa,* (London: Routledge and Kegan Paul). p. 192

32 Clapham, *Rewriting Ethiopian History*

33 After claiming that Ethiopia is merely "an extension of the Oriental world", Erlich further speaks of the emergence of Ethiopia as an "Oriental state." See H. Erlich, (1994) *Ethiopia and the Middle East,* (Boulder: Lynne Rienner Publishers). pp. 3-4

34 Clapham, *Rewriting Ethiopian History*

35, Vol. 21, No. 3, p. 144

AR

AReview of Nigerian Affairs
RNA

Annual Subscription Rates

Companies/orgs./institutions: £180
(including access to the online editions)

Individuals: online and Print: £60
Individuals: Online only: £30

Retail sales:
Individuals (print)   £20 (+ P&P)
Online   £10 per issue

To contribute, contact the journal's editor;

The Editor, (Dr Jideofor Adibe)
editor@adonis-abbey.com

Subscription enquiries
please contact: sales@adonis-abbey.com

Adonis & Abbey Publishers Ltd
P.O. Box 43418,
London
SE11 4XZ
United Kingdom
Tel.: +44 (0) 2077938893

African Renaissance
Vol. 4 No.1 Quarter 1 2007
pp66-75

Privatization Programme in Ethiopia:
Is the Cause justified?

Jesiah Selvam[1]

Introduction

Ethiopia actually began the 1990s with a clear vision of reversing the socio economic crisis of the 1980s and rapidly transforming the economy. The clear vision was nothing but the economic reforms, facilitated by the Transitional Economic Policy (TEP) which was then announced by the EPRDF (Ethiopian People's Revolutionary Democratic Front) government in November 1991. Following that policy, a three year Policy Framework Paper was also developed and agreed with the IMF and the World Bank in October 1992. The Policy Framework Paper, which forms the basis of the economic reform programme, sought to revitalize the economy and create a more market oriented economic system, giving room for privatisation and thereby, replacing the rigidly centralized command economy.

Economic reforms urged the country to review the conditions of their State Owned Enterprises (SOEs). Structural Adjustment programme in SOEs normally brings out a clear picture of what SOEs are meant for the economy of the country. In the wake of economic reforms, there have been many a good number of privatisation cases, but brought under two categories: First, if SOEs were not meaningful in the economic sense, there would be no option but to privatize. Second, even if they were sound, sadly no other option, but to privatize thanks to the conditionalities of the World Bank, IMF and other international donors. Many are perplexed in searching for the real and logical causes why many developing countries have introduced privatization programme. The debate on African privatization is hot and long standing as many African intellectuals blame the international donors for the cause. The fact is nonetheless otherwise.

This paper, therefore, attempts to examine what exactly has prompted Ethiopia to go for privatisation. In this regard, the causal analysis helps this study to ascertain through some of the selected indicators as to what factors were behind privatisation of the country. The paper has four sections: the next one discusses the background of Puss; third deals with the causal analysis and the final ends with summary along with some concluding remarks.

Background of SOEs

March of Public Sector Undertakings from 1974 to 1991

The institutional framework under which economic enterprises operated prior to 1974 was a free enterprise system with an open policy in the sense that no minimum requirement was imposed on the establishment and operation of enterprises. The role of government was mainly to encourage potential investors both from within and outside the country to commit resources in industrial investment. The economic enterprises, especially the SOEs of that time, had shown fast growth and expansion, but the growth did not continue after 1974, leaving a lesson (though it is not new) that the state is an uninspired entrepreneur and a bad manager.

After the emergence of Marxist Military government in 1974, the political philosophy changed and ownership moved toward the state. On 7th February 1975, the government released a document outlining socialist Ethiopia's economic policy. The policy identified three manufacturing areas slated for state involvement - basic industries that produced goods serving other industries and that had the capacity to create linkages in the economy; industries that produced essential goods for the general population; and industries that made drugs, medicine, tobacco and beverages. The policy also grouped the public and private sectors into activities reserved for the state, activities where state and private capital could operate jointly, and activities left to the private sector.

As a result, industrial enterprises were more affected than any other sector as the necessity of public ownership was forced especially on almost all medium and large-scale industries. In line with socializing the national properties, 87 manufacturing enterprises were nationalized in 1975. In the following few years, their number grew to 134, and by 1983 as many as 159 enterprises were nationalized. However, many of the nationalized enterprises were very old, and more than 50 percent of which were operating beyond their technically expected life, and were financially weak.

It is distressing to note that even the operating medium and large-sized enterprises declined from 479 in 1970 to 399 in 1984, owing to closures caused by their inherent structural, managerial and financial weaknesses. Altogether the experiment of Derg regime on expanding public ownership proved to be failure, owing to mismanagement and overstaffing, inappropriate investments, poor coverage and quality of services, high debt and fiscal losses and increased corruption. It was the Transitional Government that came into power in 1991 which initiated privatisation aimed at stopping this haemorrhage. In 1992, there were 211 large and medium sized manufacturing plants under state control, of which 164 were under the management of the Ministry of Industry, while the remaining 47 firms were under other ministries.

As of 2002/03, there are only 141 enterprises (large and medium industries) under public ownership, employing around 56,588 employees out of 98,136 in this sector, whereas the private sector with 769 establishments has employed 41,551 (CSA, 2003: 45). Despite the fact that privatisation has been carried out for the past ten years, the public sector seemed to be dominating in terms of the value added and number of people employed.

Initiatives and reasons for privatisation

In almost in all cases of privatisation in the Least Developed Countries (LDC), the reasons usually include (a) high fiscal pressure on governments (high budgetary deficit, large domestic public debt, and large external debt), (b) high dependency on loans from international organizations (WB and IMF), (c) a large share of SOEs in total investment, (d) inferior and poor performance of SOEs in production and profitability, and (e) lower long term growth. Many studies have shown that privatisation occurs in countries with higher financial problems, such as large budgetary deficit and external debt in percent of GDP.

In the Ethiopian context, privatisation was conceived as an important element in the transformation from a command to a market oriented economy, reduction of alarming budget deficit and external debt, injection of openness into the economy, development of the private sector at a macro level, and alleviation of problems such as managerial inefficiency and poor performance of SOEs at the micro level. It is also said that the Ethiopian government, with these objectives in mind adopted privatisation as an immediate reform measure. The next section of the study deals with causal analysis to measure the extent of causes and their validity to justify privatisation in the country.

Performance of SOEs

Privatisation has been implemented for many reasons. The first and foremost reason was the poor performance of SOEs particularly in the production and utilization of plant capacity. A rise in the number of weak SOEs and their disappointing performance in production led to their privatisation.

According to the financial reports of the Ministry of Industry, at the end of 1990/91 fiscal year, the liquidity balance of 53 enterprises was less than one, indicating that most firms could not cover their working capital requirements. It is a known fact in many countries that privatisation led to positive changes in finance and operation of the privatised enterprises.

Table 1 Classification of SOEs by Profitability, 1991/92

Sector	Profit Making	Loss Making	IIA[♦]	Total
Industry	63	40	10	113
Agriculture	8	20	9	37
Mining and Energy	2	2	1	5
Construction	6	5	7	18
Transport and Commodity	10	2	1	13
Housing	1	0	4	5
Trade	10	1	3	4
Hotels and Tourism	5	2	1	8
Health	3	0	0	3
Finance	4	1	0	5
Others	2	0	1	3
Total*	114(50.9)	73(32.6)	37(16.5)	224(100)

Note: *Figure given in the parentheses indicate the percentage in the column total

[♦] Information Inadequate

Source: MoI (1992)

Table 1 indicates that as of 1991/92, 33 percent of a total number of SOEs, including small sized enterprises were under the category of loss-making enterprises, in which industries accounted for 55 percent while agriculture constituted 27 percent (MoI, 1992) resulting in the widening the deficit in federal budgets. Obviously, this reason may justify the government privatizing its SOEs. Gupta et al. (2001) support such justification to privatize if the government cares about efficiency. But Guo and Yao (2005) argue that efficiency is not a concern in the government's decision on privatisation because an unprofitable firm may still be able to deliver taxes to the government and maintain sizable employment.

Moreover, the GDP by industrial sector (at constant factor cost) over the period of 1986/87-1991/92 was reduced from USD714.29 million to USD326.93 million (MoFED, 2003). A high slash in the Gross Value of Output (GVO) made the average growth rate to be negative 3.8 percent in 1987/88, which was raised to the same negative growth but of highest standing at 19.1 in 1991/92. Such a bad show cannot be justified with the political uncertainties that reached their highest point in1990/91. This shows that poor performance in the overall industrial GVO was mainly due to the structural and managerial incapability of SOEs. Hence, it is found that the rise in the number of weak SOEs and their dismal performance in GVO may be one of the strong reasons for privatizing SOEs in the country.

Capacity Utilisation of SOEs

Capacity utilisation is one of the factors determining the viability of SOEs in a country. Capacity utilisation in this regard is analysed to justify the need for privatisation.

Table 2 Capacity Utilisation of SOEs

Sub Sector	1987/88	1988/89	1989/90	1990/91	1991/92
Food	83.9	93	97.2	69.3	41.8
Beverage	100.2	94.8	83.5	60	53.5
Tobacco	81.4	74.8	68.3	72.8	51.2
Textile	87.3	72.9	82.8	52.2	36.2
Leather	99.0	105.7	95.0	67.2	59.1
Wood	106.2	102.7	99.6	78.0	87.9
Non-Metal	99.7	104.9	83.7	80.3	66.5
Printing	100	98.0	92.8	94.2	93.6
Chemical	96.2	85.7	87.4	41.8	39.6
Metal	37.6	28.1	19.8	11.6	7.1
Average (In Percentage)	**82.2**	**78.8**	**76.5**	**54**	**40.9**

Source: MoPED (1994)

Table 2 analyses the capacity utilisation in SOEs over the period 1987/88-1991/92 and shows a poor performance in the utilisation of business capacity. Except printing and wood industry, others showed a dismaying performance over the period. Food and beverage industries, which constitute a major portion in the economy, were no exception to this trend.

The capacity utilisation of food industries which stood at 83.9 percent in 1987/88, declined to 41.8 percent in 1991/92, whereas the beverage section had a decrease of 50 percent over the same period and the same case was approximately found in other sub-sectors of industry such as tobacco, textile, leather, wood, non-metal and chemical. The overall capacity utilisation of the Ethiopian industries in fact declined by 50 percent, i.e. it was cut down from 82.2 percent in 1987/88 to 40.9 percent in 1991/92. Most of the industries with a high share in manufacturing production operated below 50 percent of their respective attainable capacity (MoPED, 1994).

At the end of 1999/00, the major loss making SOEs registered over USD 23.44 million losses, out of which 54.8 percent was in state farms while 25 percent was in industry. In a market- oriented economy, the motive force behind production is profit. To the contrary, the profit motive was choked off from the SOEs in the past and present eventually leaving them at the point of collapse.

The above discussion proves that the poor performance, under capacity utilization and financial loss of SOEs created scepticism about the ability of the government to manage and operate enterprises efficiently. This study shows that mismanagement, shortage of raw materials and spare- parts, inadequate allocation of foreign exchange, non-overhauled and outdated machineries were among the major reasons for this disappointing performance (see also Tefera, 1993). Out of these reasons, the shortage of raw materials and inadequate allocation of foreign exchange may not be the inherent problems of SOEs. Unless the government liberalizes its financial and trade protection, a higher performance would not have been possible even for the private sector. Other major reasons to privatize were said to be the wider budget deficit (Fekru, 1993) and heavy debt burden.

Budgetary Deficit and External Debt

Studies have confirmed that one of the main reasons for budget deficit was the money the government spent aimlessly in the name of renovation and rehabilitation of SOEs, which resulted in no returns. It will be fair to assume that had the government neither borrowed the money from the external funding agencies nor spent such in weakened SOEs, it would have narrowed the budget deficit.

Budget deficit-GDP ratio, which stood at 0.069 in 1986/87, jumped to 0.097 in 1991/92 (MoPED, 2003). Deficit to GDP ratio shows how much the GDP should contribute to compensate the gap between the federal revenues and expenditure, that is, in the GDP of 1986/87, 6.9 cents of every USD was additionally required to balance the budget, that is, the revenue equals expenditure, whereas in 1991/92, it was 9.7 cents extra needed for every single USD of GDP to arrive at a zero-deficit budget. Over this period, the deficit/GDP grew at the average rate of 0.112 percent with standard deviation of 0.0237.

The national debt is perennially at the centre of economic policy debates. In recent years, the government's expenditures have abundantly overtaken the revenues which make the budgetary position so pathetic that the government is forced to borrow from external sources. As for

Ethiopia, budget deficit and poverty have become the most critical challenges, the effect of which negatively turns out the country to highly indebted. The pattern of Ethiopian external debt had changed into a bad fashion after the Imperial government was overthrown by the Derg regime.

During its 17 year tenure, the Derg government increased the country's total debt by 30 fold, owing not only to its extravagant spending but also to the high expenditure on SOEs due to an increase in government interventions in the economy. It is also found that as of 1991/92, defence expenditure accounted for 31 percent of the total expenditure, whereas the government's expenditure on SOEs took a share of 4 percent in the total expenditure shown in the budget (MoFED, 2003). Eventually, the annual average of external debt for the period 1974/1975-1983/84 stood at USD1,656 million which became USD9,341million in 1991/92.

The syndrome analysis clearly exhibits a burden of external debt in relation to GDP of the country. The debt/GDP ratio stood at an alarming rate of 0.98 and 1.30 in the fiscal years 1987/88 and 1991/92 respectively. Over the period, the debt/GDP ratio grew at the average rate of 1.04 with standard deviation 0.12367. The analysis shows that no significant debt reduction was made over the period.

Figure 1

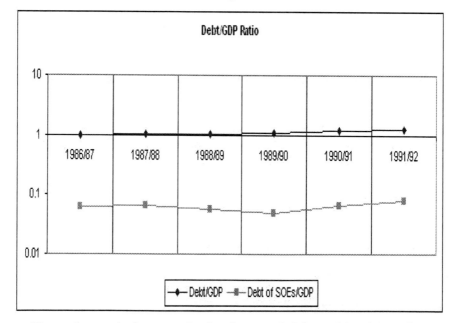

Figure 1 reveals the magnitude of external debt and its share of SOEs. The external debt of SOEs/GDP ratio which stood at 0.062 in the fiscal year 1986/87, increased to the ratio 0.08 with an annual average increase of 6.6 percent. This type of burden is too heavy for a government which is heavily indebted. This empirical finding shows that these SOEs are not only inefficient themselves, but also do encroach upon the fund that is meant for other developmental activities.

Summary and conclusion

Among all causes analyzed, the declining trend of industrial output and capacity utilization of SOEs in the pre-privatisation period may be the major causes at micro level behind the privatisation of SOEs in the country. The growth rate of industrial output stood at 5.57 percent below zero level and capacity utilization recorded only 55.4 percent. Profitability was reduced from 114 percent in 1986/87 to a negative 24 percent in 1991/92 which reduced the annual average growth rate to 69.83 over the period. The steady growth in the debt of SOEs/GDP may also be another haunting cause why privatisation was necessitated.

Table 3
Summary of Privatisation Causal Analysis, 1986/87-1991/92

Major Syndromes	Year						
	1986/87	1987/88	1988/89	1989/90	1990/91	1991/92	Annual Average
Industry's GVO (Growth Rate)	8	-3.8	-6.7	-4.7	-19.1	-7.1	-5.57
Capacity Utilization	Na*	82.2	78.8	76.5	54	40.9	55.4
Profitability**	114	128	119	65	17	-24	69.83
Budget Deficit/GDP Ratio***	0.069	0.088	0.112	0.138	0.113	0.097	0.088
Debt/GDP Ratio****	0.98	1.03	1.04	1.1	1.22	1.3	1.3
Debt of SOEs/GDP Ratio	0.062	0.066	0.055	0.048	0.064	0.08	0.064

Note: *Not available **As a percentage of Net Sales

***Budget Deficit excluding grants ****Debt indicates the external debt

Source: MoI (1992), MoPED (1994), World Bank (1997) & MoFED (2003b)

Moreover, the macroeconomic structural objectives such as reduction of budget deficit and external debt, which were found to be strong obstacles in the pre-privatisation period, were aimed to be brought down after the privatization of SOEs. The ratio of budget deficit and external debt to GDP that recorded 0.088 and 1.3 respectively over the period may be the other strong macro reasons for causing the country to adopt privatisation. Having analyzed the major macro and micro indicators, it was found that neither visible comparative advantages of retaining PSUs nor strategic significance of continuing public ownership may be justified.

Furthermore, the pressure of the WB and IMF as external factors may not be ruled out for implementing privatisation programme because the country's dependence on these institutions was found to be very high. Empirical evidence indicates a high degree of dependency of the African economy on external finance, particularly those provided by the WB and the IMF, indicating a positive correlation between the implementation of privatisation and dependency on loans from international organizations. But, Ethiopia would not fall completely in this category as the cause for privatization has been justified owing to the bad-syndromes of state owned enterprises.

References

CSA (2003) "Report on Large and Medium Scale Manufacturing and Electricity Industries Survey", Statistical Bulletin 281, October, (Central Statistical Authority), Addis Ababa: CSA.

Fekru, D. (1993) "Privatisation in Sub-Saharan Africa: Origins, Trends, and Influences on Development Strategies", New Jersey: Centre for Economic Research on Africa (CERAF), p.3.

Guo, K. and Yao, Y. (2005) "Causes of Privatisation in China: Testing Several Hypothesies", The Economics of Transition", Vol. 13, no. 2, pp.211-38.

Gupta, N., Ham, J. and Svejnar, J. (2001) "Priorities and Sequencing in Privatisation: Theory and Evidence from the Czech Republic", Working Paper No. 323-1, University of Michigan Business School, William Davidson Institute, pp. 1-32.

MoFED (2003) Economic Indicators, Department of Policy Analysis, Addis Ababa: MoFED.

MoI (1992) "Industrial Restructuring in Ethiopia", Vol. I, August, Addis Ababa: MoI, pp. 21-4.

MoPED (1994) "Survey of Current Economic Conditions in Ethiopia", Vol. II, no. 1, February, Addis Ababa: MoPED, p.2-9.

Tefera, A.H. (1993) "Privatisation Initiative in Ethiopia", , September 1993, Addis Ababa: Ministry of Industry, p. 26

World Bank (1997) African Development Indicators, Washington, D.C.: World Bank.

Dr. Jesiah Selvam is Director, Indian Academy School of Management Studies, Bangalore-560 043, India. He formerly served as faculty member in Debub University, Ministry of Education, Ethiopia; Tel. 0091-80-25444103/25442370; email: sjesiah@yahoo.com

African Renaissance
Vol. 4 No.1 Quarter 1 2007
pp76-80

The Role of Indigenous Medicinal Plants in Ethiopian Healthcare

Fekadu Fullas, RPh, PhD

Introduction

In today's world of evidence-based medicine, the old system of traditional medicine has been scrutinized very closely, and rightly so, from the scientific angle in an attempt to render it more amenable to systematic investigation. In fact, looking back in time, modern medicine has benefited a lot from traditional medicine in that the latter had provided key leads emanating from folkloric uses of medicinal plants. A large array of modern pharmaceutical agents has been derived from such leads, which were eventually traced back to traditional uses of medicinal plants. Consequently, substances such as the antimalarial quinine, the decongestant pseudoephedrine, the pain killer codeine, just to name a few, were discovered as a result of ethnobotanical information obtained from traditional uses of plants, which are the natural "manufacturing houses" of these drugs. Plants continue to play a major role in providing prototype molecules for possible development into conventional drugs by the pharmaceutical industry. This article deals with the role played by medicinal plants in healthcare in Ethiopia against a backdrop of condensed history. It also provides synopses of select Ethiopian medicinal plants, and concludes by pointing out the future role that they can play as a source of enhanced herbal products.

History and Current Status

A cursory look at the history of the use of traditional medicine (especially of medicinal plants) in Ethiopia reveals that such use dates back to the time of the Axumite kingdom, if not to earlier periods. Many manuscripts attesting to this fact, and which are now in the custody of the Ethiopian National Traditional Medicine Preparation and Therapy Association, have been recovered. They mention, among other traditional practices, that a large number of medicinal plants were used. The manuscripts claim that during the era of the Axumite kingdom (7th-11th C), about 8,000 plants

76

were used as medicinal agents. This period was followed by the Zagwe dynasty (11th-13th C), during which time about 2,800 medicinal plants were recorded to have been used. Similarly, during the era of Gondarine kingdom (1636-1865), medicinal plants numbering some 2,900 were employed. A manuscript was also recovered from the ruins of Aba Jifar's palace in Jimma during the era of King Menelik II over 100 years ago. It included about 589 plants which were used as therapeutic agents. Close to 700 medicinal plants were also recorded to have been used during the reigns of King Hailemelekot through Emperor Haile Selassie I (1870-1974). In each of the above manuscripts, a lesser number of other medicinal agents of animal and mineral origins were also presented. It is worth noting that the number of plants may have been exaggerated, especially in the older manuscripts, considering the fact that only about 7,500 plant species are known to exist in Ethiopia today. It is also possible that many of the plants may have been counted more than once. This may be true even after allowing for plant species that could have been extinct since the times of the manuscripts. In any event, it is clear that medicinal plants played a pivotal role in the treatment of various afflictions.

More recently, several publications which listed currently used Ethiopian medicinal plants have appeared. In 1971, Tsehai Berhane Selassie authored an annotated paper based on an earlier manuscript by Grazmach Gebrewold Aregawi of Dega Damot, which described the uses of over 200 plants. In addition, the paper included a description of magic and rituals used in some of the healing processes. In 1973, the Polish Stephen Strelcyn produced a book listing the medical applications of 300 plants. A few years later, in 1976 a mimeograph was published by the University of Addis Ababa, based on extensive field and herbarium studies. This work listed the geographic origins of about 250 medicinal plants along with their uses. A landmark book titled Este Debdabe was published in 1989 by Gelahun Abate, with Sebsebe Demissew as the editor. This publication in turn included descriptions of over 250 medicinal herbs. Most recently, a comprehensive book authored by Dawit Abate and Ahadu Ayehu came out in 1993. The book elaborated the uses of about 240 medicinal plants. Since 2001, a few critical books dealing with various aspects of Ethiopian medicinal plants have been published.

Presently, there are anywhere between 650 and 1,000 medicinal plants in Ethiopia, comprising about 10 per cent of the entire flowering plants found in the country. However, perhaps the more commonly used medicinal plants may number in the vicinity of 200. Many of these plants have not been investigated scientifically, although they have been used by the population for a long time. A common argument advanced in favor of continuity of use of such long-used plants is that people would have dropped them if they hadn't worked, and therefore they should have been effective to be sustained for such a long time. However, that reasoning doesn't suffice to promote rational use of phytomedicines. Scientific studies encompassing chemistry, pharmacology, formulation and standardization are required not only to justify the use of botanicals (when there are cases to justify), but also to produce refined, convenient, and quality-controlled   products.

It has been widely claimed that about 80% of Ethiopians rely on traditional medicine (predominantly medicinal plants) to treat their illnesses and maintain their health. This is more true in rural than urban areas. Even in urban areas people are inclined to use so-called home remedies to treat common illness symptoms. In such cases, accurate diagnoses of diseases, and expertise in preparing and administering herbal medications may not be usually required. In this category of conditions fall such disease states as taeniasis, stomach conditions, skin problems, and symptoms such as headache, cold, cough, and diarrhea. People have treated these conditions for hundreds (maybe even thousands) of years by using traditional ways. They have been successful in most cases in alleviating their suffering by concocting various preparations derived from medicinal herbs which abounded in their environs. More serious medical problems were usually deferred to "expert" traditional medical practitioners, or modern physicians as the case may be.

Ethiopian traditional medicine consists of various treatment modalities, but the bulk of it employs medicinal plants as part of the treatment regimens. Consistent with the prevailing thoughts of the time, many of the old treatment methods were, as can be expected, steeped in magico-religious beliefs. As time went by, traditional medicine started receiving fresh perspectives. A number of medicinal plants have survived scientific scrutiny to varying degrees.

Select Ethiopian Medicinal Plants

There are a number of Ethiopian medicinal plants which have undergone scientific investigation. These plants have been used in traditional medicine to treat various ailments. In the following section, an abridged sampling of those remedies is given.

1. Dingetegna (*Taverniera abyssinica*): This all-Ethiopian traditional plant has been used to treat sudden illness characterized by fever and stomachache. Both uses of the plant have been investigated scientifically, and the conclusions support them.

2. Endod (*Phytolacca dodecandra*): This plant is best known for its use in the control of schistosomiasis which claims thousands of lives in Ethiopia every year. Although various parts of the plant are used directly by humans for diseases such as ascariasis, gonorrhea, malaria, rabies, syphilis, etc., *endod* berries are used as a molluscicidal agent to help arrest the spread of the infection by disrupting the transmission cycle.

3. Metere (*Glinus lotoides*): Of more than 2 dozen plants that are known to

be used for tapeworm infestation (taeniasis), recently *metere* seems to have received more chemical and biological investigations. The taenicidal activity of the plant has been attributed to its saponin constituents. The plant has also been shown to be relatively safe and effective.
4. Gizawa (*Withania somnifera*): In Ethiopia, this plant is used for joint infection, arthritis, and malaria. Studies have shown that it indeed exhibits antibiotic, anti-inflammatory and antimalarial activities. These findings are in support of similar uses of the plant in Ethiopian traditional medicine.
5. Gulo zeit (*Ricinus communis*): Among other uses of the plant, the oil from the seeds is used in Ethiopia as a purgative to soften the digestive tract. Castor oil is commonly used in modern medicine to cleanse the gut prior to medical procedures. It is no wonder then that the oil from this plant is used in Ethiopian traditional medicine as a purgative.
6. Bahr zaf (*Eucalyptus spp.*): Although there are over 55 species of Eucalyptus in Ethiopia, Eucalyptus globulus is the most abundant species. Apart from its immense economic utility, Eucalyptus is also used as a medicinal agent. The vapor obtained from boiling the leaves is inhaled as a common household remedy to treat common cold symptoms. In conventional medicine, the oil obtained from the leaves is used to make ointments and cough preparations.

The above few examples go to show clearly that the uses of a number of Ethiopian medicinal plants are supported by scientific studies, or parallel uses in modern medicine. There is also a vast botanical resource yet to be investigated for possible application in enhanced traditional medicine.

Future Prospects

It is obvious that Ethiopian medicinal plants are a rich source of many remedies. In a country where modern health services are out of reach for about 80% of the population, these plants provide an alternative ammunition to fight a number of diseases. Even with the future expansion of modern health services to cover the underserved section of the population, it is quite conceivable that, if properly harnessed, botanical remedies can provide a complementary source to modern medication supply. In order to ensure their sustainability, Ethiopian medicinal plants need to be conserved, lest they be endangered and eventually be extinct as a result of unbridled deforestation and natural calamities. A sound conservation program aimed at preserving this rich biota is a pre-requisite. Along with such a program, the foundation of a light modern botanical products industry needs to be laid down. Policy makers need to provide legislative and infra-structural support to entrepreneurs who may wish to invest in businesses to develop medicinal plant products.

Conclusions

That Ethiopia has a vast resource of medicinal plants is incontrovert-ible. The question is how to streamline this resource for the benefit of not only those people who do not have access to modern medicines, but also for those also who fail on conventional medications, or those, who for economic reasons opt for local products which can potentially be as effective. As shown in the examples above, there are botanical remedies which are indeed effective, but which can be standardized and produced in modern dosage forms such as liquids, tablets, ointments. For this to materialize, a concerted effort is required by scientists and entrepreneurs, along with governmental legislative and infra-structural support. If this is realized, then it will obviously earn foreign exchange savings for the country, in addition to opening up new economic opportunities for investors. As a result, Ethiopian scientists (botanists, agriculturalists, chemists, pharma-cologists, clinicians, and other researchers) will also be motivated to engage in applied and impact-driven research in this untapped virgin field. The potential contribution of enhanced Ethiopian medicinal products to the healthcare of the population, and derivatively to the economy of the country is indeed enormous.

Key References:

Berhane Selassie, T. (1971). An Ethiopian Medical Text-Book, Written by Gerazmach Gebrawld Aragahn, Daga Damot. Journal of Ethiopian Studies IX (1): 95-180.

Strelcyn, S. (1973). Medicines et. Plantes D'Ethiopie. Instituto Universitario Orientale, Napoli.

Abate, G. [edited by Demissew, S] (1989). Etse Debdabe (Ethiopian Traditional Medicine). Biology Department, Addis Ababa University.

Abebe, D. and Ayehu, A. (1993). Medicinal Plants and Enigmatic Health Practices of Northern Ethiopia. B.S.P.E., Addis Ababa.

Zewdu, M. and Demissie, A. (2001). Conservation and Sustainable Use of Medicinal Plants in Ethiopia. Institute of Biodiversity Conservation and Research, Addis Ababa.

Fullas, F. (2001). Ethiopian Traditional Medicine: Common Medicinal Plants in Perspective. Sioux City, IA (USA).

Fullas, F. (2003). Spice Plants in Ethiopia: Their Culinary and Medicinal Applications, Sioux City, IA (USA).

Fekadu Fullas, RPh, PhD has authored over 40 publications, including a book chapter and 3 books)

To contribute to
African Renaissance
please contact:
editor@adonis-abbey.com

African Renaissance
Vol. 4 No.1 Quarter 1 2007
pp82-90

Summoning Osagyefo Kwame Nkrumah

Solomon Gomes

Introduction

On the eve of the 50th Anniversary of the independence of Ghana a ministerial meeting convened at the Commission of the African Union in November 2006, to discuss the establishment of a United States of Africa – a single government for the entire continent. Deja vu! The tone of the debate mirrored the debate that took place in Accra, in 1965. What was regrettably clear was the fact that there was no institutional memory. Had such a memory continued to exist such a meeting would never have convened. Most shocking, however, was the fact that none of the Commissioners, Ministers present and their Ambassadors had any clue about the 1965 Accra Summit debate over the issue of Union Government for Africa. The ministerial meeting gave truth to two African sayings: The first, "those who do not remember the mistakes of the past are bound to repeat them in the future." The second: "if you do not know where you came from you cannot know where you are going."

The 50th Anniversary of the independence of Ghana is an historic milestone that requires reflection not only on the part of Ghanaians but all of Africa. Nkrumha's political thoughts are still with us and the more we study them the more informed we become about Kwame Nkrumah as an extraordinary and committed standard bearer of the Pan African ideal.

This paper focuses on the Accra Summit of the Organization of African Unity (OAU) of 1965, the general debate over the proposals tabled by host-President, Osagyefo Kwame Nkrumah and Mwalimu Julius Neyrere's take on that otherwise forgotten historic Summit of African Heads of State and Government. This summit convened two years after the OAU was established and as Mwalimu Nyerere recalled it was not well remembered.

The Accra Summit of 1965

The 1965 OAU summit was the Third Ordinary session of the Assembly of Heads of State and Government and Kwame Nkrumah chose to table his proposal for an organ to respond to developments during times when the OAU organs were not in session. Kwame Nkrumah was a visionary. Kwame Nkrumah advanced a strong argument for a multi-purpose mechanism that would ensure that decisions of the OAU were implemented, and could respond to threats to international peace and security in Africa, when the organs of the Organization were not in session.

The full expression of political will on the part of the participants at the 1965 Accra Summit was at best conflicting and at worst, selfish. It was Kwame Nkrumah's conviction that a single (Union) Government for Africa was the best weapon the African States could have in an international milieu where the strong states would always seek to dominate and exploit the weak ones. Kwame Nkrumah was wrongly and deliberately portrayed by western media as the aspirant President, of "Union Government for Africa." The vision of Kwame Nkrumah was revolutionary. It aimed to reverse the unsanctioned 1885 historical partition of Africa by European imperial and colonial powers. He saw Africa's resurgence in a single continental entity.

Conceptually, and from the perspective of many African delegations at the 1965 Accra summit, the proposal was seen as a call for an end to sovereignty and national independence. This was considered a bigger threat than the weak status the newly independent African States had in the international system. The proposal was resisted for two reasons. The first was that Kwame Nkrumah did not foresee the hostile reception his proposal would receive from erstwhile colonial Governments and the United States that were engaged in Cold War politics. The slogan "Africa for the Africans" was unacceptable to the Governments that mistakenly concluded that it was a communist inspired campaign. It was consequently perceived as meaning the elimination of European/American influence in Africa, a view that was considered dangerous to their interests in Africa.

This was the international milieu the African States found themselves. The continuing influence of the former colonial powers in Africa meant that some African States had been influenced to oppose or reject the proposals at the Accra Summit. . The debate at the Accra Summit was an important milestone in the life of an organization that was barely two years old. The significance of the Accra debate was that it brought to the fore, "revolutionary" and "conservative" proclivities in relation to the proposals before them.

A number of African Heads of State that had expressed support for the creation of an "Executive Council" based their arguments in part, on Article 2 Paragraph 2(f) of the OAU Charter, which outlined, that "in fulfilling the purposes of the Organization, the Member States shall coordinate and harmonize their general policies, especially, in defense and security". The latter, they argued, could best be done within such a body.

They also cited Article 8 of the Charter, to make the case for the establishment of an "Executive Council": The Assembly of Heads of State and Government shall be the supreme organ of the Organization. It shall, subject to the provisions of the Charter, discuss matters of common concern to Africa with a view to coordinating and harmonizing the general policy of the Organization. It may in addition review the structure, functions, and acts of all the organs and any specialized agencies which may be created in accordance with the present Charter."[i]

The opponents of the proposal for such a "Council" argued in turn, that such a body would, among other things, infringe on the sovereignty of the Member States, and that Article 8 did not as a matter of legal fact, give authority for the setting up of another organ, especially, along the lines proposed".[ii] The debate that ensued provided an insight into what the political thinking was in 1965. One delegation even suggested that in lieu of the "Executive Council" the General Secretariat should play the role envisaged for it. Another delegation suggested that a Committee should be set up to study the idea and submit appropriate recommendations to the next Summit. Yet, another still argued, that there was no need to amend the two-year old Charter.[iii]

There was another suggestion, that the functions envisaged for the Executive Council should be delegated to the OAU Secretary-General. However, the Assembly of Heads and Government were not disposed at that time, to giving the Secretary-General any political authority. His role was defined as an "Administrative Secretary-General", restricting him from the political management of affairs that fell within the purview of the Council of Ministers. President Ahmed Sekou Toure of Guinea asserted during the debate, that neither an Executive Council nor the General Secretariat could be more than what the Assembly wanted it to be.

To allay the fear of those who considered the idea of an Executive Council a threat to sovereignty, he argued that the Council could not be a threat to the sovereignty of the Member States. This is how he explained it:

> "Those who would be charged with the implementation of decisions of the Assembly would have less authority than the Assembly, which makes the decisions. The Executive is a shadow of the OAU. The OAU exists, it decides and its decisions must be implemented. Action is but the shadow of the decision, and consequently, the Executive is the shadow of our decisions. We should have no fear."[iv]

The raison d'etre of Nkrumah's proposal was linked with his understanding of the colonial history of Africa. In the public lecture he delivered in Accra in 1997, marking the 40th anniversary of the independence of Ghana and three years before he passed away, Mwalimu Julius Nyerere the former President of Tanzania, recalled the atmosphere of that important and yet unsung Third Ordinary Summit of the Assembly of Heads of State and Government in 1965, in Accra. He informed his audience as follows,

"...That Summit is not well remembered as the founding summit in 1963, or the Cairo summit of 1964. The fact that Kwame Nkrumah did not last long as Head of State of Ghana after that Summit may have contributed to the comparative obscurity of that important Summit. But I want to suggest that the reason why we do not talk about that Summit is probably psychological; it was a failure. That failure still haunts us today."[v]

What was the failure?

Mwalimu Julius Nyerere provided an insight into the thoughts of the founding fathers, in this excerpt:

"What the founding fathers – certainly a hard core of them – had in mind was genuine desire to move Africa forwards greater unity. We loathed balkanization of the continent into small unviable states, most of which had borders, which did not make ethnic of geographical sense. The Cairo Declaration of 1964 was promoted by a profound realization of the absurdity of inherited borders. It was quite clear that some adventurers would try to change those borders by force of arms. Indeed, it was already happening. Ethiopia and Somalia were at war over inherited colonial borders.'"

From the above perspective, Mwalimu Julius Nyerere focused attention on host President Kwame Nkrumah: Kwame Nkrumah was opposed to balkanization as much as he was opposed to colonialism in Africa. To him and to a number of us, the two – Balkanization and Colonialism – were twins, genuine liberation of Africa had to attack both twins. A struggle against colonialism must go hand-in-hand with a struggle against balkanization of Africa. The mechanism Kwame Nkrumah had in mind was an integral part of his radical proposal: Union Government for Africa. A number of Heads of State shared Kwame Nkrumah's view of "Union Government for Africa" and for the "Mechanism" he had in mind.

There were those of course, who did not appreciate his proposals that subsequently set the stage for the debate that followed. As host-President, Osagyefo Kwame Nkrumah seized the opportunity to table his proposal of an "Executive Council". His argument in favor of this new body was that the OAU needed, as he put it, "an apt and effective machinery to put teeth into our Organization." [vi] He foresaw the "Executive Council" as composed of Heads of State and Government that "would become an arm of the Assembly of Heads of State and Government, and be responsible for initiating policies and making recommendations."[vii]

Kwame Nkrumah wanted the "Executive Council" to be empowered to initiate action in the event of inter-state disputes or conflicts in the continent, and especially, when the Organization was not in session. He wanted, in short, a mechanism to fill what he considered a "void" in between meetings of the Organs of the OAU. Kwame Nkrumah wished to draw attention to what he perceived as a "void" in the Organization. He illustrated this, by reminding the Summit, that according to Rule 9 of the Rules of Procedure of the OAU Assembly of Heads of State and Government they were only able to meet once a year: the Assembly shall meet only once a year. That was in his view, a serious limitation that had to be addressed.

Kwame Nkrumah argued, that there was a need for "prompt and effective action" [on the part of the OAU], in dealing with threats to international peace and security in Africa. The Assembly of Heads of State and Government could not do so if it met once a year. The language he used was borrowed from Article 24 paragraph 1 of the Charter of the United Nations. Kwame Nkrumah also felt, that convening extra-ordinary sessions of the Assembly of Heads of State and Government was time consuming and inadequate.

Nkrumah's argument was very persuasive and he was correct in his assessment that the convening of extra-ordinary sessions of the OAU required the consent of two-thirds majority of the Member States, which would take a lot of time to obtain. Sending telex messages to African capitals was a slow process with no guarantees a response would be immediate. The argument was basically that getting two-thirds of the Membership to give their consent would consume a lot of time during which a conflict could escalate and militate against efforts to manage it.

Nkrumah believed that the most practical option for the African Heads of State and Government was a "Mechanism" or what he called an "Executive Council" that would function on a continuous basis, along the lines of the Security Council and respond to conflicts at short notice. It would also ensure that the resolutions and decisions of the Summit were implemented in a timely fashion.

The "Executive Council" Nkrumah had in mind was to be headed by a "full time Chairman" (a sitting Head of State), appointed by his peers to oversee a Council composed of eight other Heads of State "who would work on a part-time basis". This was how he explained it:

> Under my proposal, the Assembly of Heads of State and Government shall continue to be the supreme governing body of the OAU as in Article VIII of our Charter. I further propose that the Assembly shall elect a Chair President and a number of Union Vice Presidents to meet periodically during the ensuing year in order to review the work of the Executive Council when the Assembly is not in session. The General Secretariat of the OAU shall be the Secretariat of the Executive Council.

The intent was to have a Mechanism that would function continually, and fill the void in between summit meetings of the Organization of African Unity. It would address urgent issues including, serious disputes between the Member States. Nkrumah rationalized, that such a Mechanism would fill the void and transform the OAU from being an organization that reacts to disputes and conflicts to one that was pro-active and effective. The proposal did not address questions such as where the "Executive Council" would be located, the frequency of meetings or whether a sitting Head of State could assume such a responsibility.

The unfortunate element that militated against Nkrumah's proposal of an "Executive Council" was linking it to a radical proposal that was his foremost political objective, namely, the establishment of: "Union Government for Africa". While a majority of the African delegations at the 1965 Accra Summit were politely receptive to the proposal for an "Executive Council, they were extremely reticent about "Union Government for Africa."

A few delegations were from the very start, vehemently, but quietly opposed to "Union Government for Africa". Some felt that the proposal would push the OAU to move faster. Others felt that what was needed was a slow process of integration that would evolve within the regions of Africa: the precursor of the Regional Economic Community of the 1980s and 1990s. Nkrumah saw "unity in strength".

The political environment of Africa at the time was characterized by a wider political conservatism. The conservative African leaders who were not enthused about "Union Government for Africa" constituted the majority in Accra. While they saw merit for a "mechanism" to fill the void in between meetings of the organs of the OAU, they were not inclined to embrace a radical idea like Union Government of Africa -- that would threaten their newly won independence and respective status as Heads of State and Government. They out-numbered the leaders with radical political proclivities who were supportive of the proposals.

Mwalimu Julius Nyerere explained the reason why some of his peers were opposed or reluctant to embrace the proposals of Kwame Nkrumah: Once you multiply National Anthems, National Flags and National Passports, seats at the United Nations and individuals entitled to 21 gun salute, not to speak of a host of Ministers, Prime Ministers and Envoys, you would have a whole army of powerful people with invested interests in keeping Africa balkanized. That was what Nkrumah encountered in 1965. The majority of Kwame Nkrumah's peers saw the end of their respective status as Heads of independent States.

Mwalimu Julius Nyerere confirmed that a number of founding fathers had a genuine desire at that time to move Africa towards greater unity. The overwhelming view among the African leaders at the Accra Summit, however, was that "Union Government for Africa" was an idea whose time had not come. It was in short, a premature radical political proposition. The odds against "Union Government for Africa" were consequently, great but not insurmountable.

Kwame Nkrumah envisioned a radical political transformation of the

African continent. His proposals made a lot of sense: amalgamate and consolidate African Unity, and eventually, eliminate the balkanized status of post-colonial Africa. This proposal was threat to the interests of the former Colonial powers, France and the United Kingdom in particular. Their common position of opposition to Nkrumah's proposals was understandable. As former colonial powers, France and the United Kingdom had a single aim, to frustrate Nkrumah's efforts for a united Africa by any and all means. Cold War influences were brought to bear on African Leaders during that Summit.

From a practical standpoint, the establishment of "Union Government for Africa" would have been a complex and demanding undertaking, given the continued interest of the former colonial powers in the continued balkanization and weakness of the African States on the one hand, and the issue of which States would get what, and who would be the Head of "Union Government in Africa) on the other?

The 1965 OAU Summit debate over the creation of an Executive Council and Union Government for Africa reflected the radical and conservative political tendencies in the Organization. It also highlighted the contrasts in perception among the Member States about how they should proceed as an association of States towards "African Unity."

At the conclusion of the 1965 debate, the Assembly of Heads of State and Government considered two draft resolutions that were respectively, submitted by the delegations of Senegal and Ghana (two opposed political tendencies): The draft resolution submitted by Senegal read in part, as follows:

> "The Assembly of Heads of State and Government meeting in Accra, Ghana from 21-25 October 1965,
> Having heard the various points of view expressed during the Assembly on the proposal to set-up an Executive Organ of the OAU,
> Convinced, that the problem requires more detailed examination,
> Decides, to create an appropriate committee to examine the various aspects and implications of the proposal and report to the Third Ordinary Session of the Assembly of Heads of State and Government"[viii]

The draft resolution Ghana submitted read in part:

> "... Takes Note of the proposal of the Government of Ghana concerning the establishment of an Executive Body of the OAU, as well as, the discussion that followed,
> Requests, Governments of the Member States of the OAU to examine that program in order to express their opinion at the next session of the Assembly"[ix]

The "Executive Council" that Kwame Nkrumah had in mind would have had three main functions:

* To deal with disputes and conflict situations in Africa;
* To ensure the maintenance of peace and security in the African continent;
* To ensure the implementation of resolutions, declarations and decisions of the Assembly of Heads of State and Government [x]

The draft resolution that Senegal tabled was unanimously adopted. The end result was that the OAU never established "a Committee to study and report to the Assembly of Heads of State and Government". The Accra summit was unwilling to countenance President Nkrumah's proposal of an "Executive Council", even though it had merit, as well as, Union Government for Africa.

The two proposals by Nkrumah were radical ideas ahead of their time. Mwalimu Julius Nyerere noted the reaction of one Head of State who attended the Accra Summit, and it summed up the disposition of many of the African leaders that were present in Accra in 1965:

> After the failure to establish a Union Government at the Accra Summit of 1965, I heard one Head of State express with relief that he was happy to be returning home to his country still Head of State. To this day, I cannot tell you whether he was serious or joking. But he may well have been serious because Kwame Nkrumah was very serious and the fear of a number of us to lose our precious status was quite palpable.[xi]

Conclusion

Fifty years after the independence of Ghana what has Africa learnt? The building blocs for a possible Union Government for Africa are the Regional Economic Communities (RECs), provided there is a proliferation of inclusive democratic political systems that put a premium on good governance, respect for the rule of law, the protection and promotion of human rights, and the promotion of peace, security and stability within and between the African States.

References

[i] Source: OAU- Charter and Rules of Procedure of the Organization of African Unity, 1963,

[ii] Source: OAU document "Verbatim Records, the 1965 Accra Summit, Op. Cit.

[iii] Ibid.

[iv] Ibid.

[v] For full details, see "Pick Up the Torch" by Mwalimu Julius K. Nyerere

in Resolving Conflicts

[vi] Source: OAU- <u>Verbatim Records of the Proceedings at the Third Ordinary session of the Assembly of Heads of State and Government,</u> Accra, Ghana, 1965 (OAU Archives).

[vii] Ibid.

[viii] Ibid.

[ix] Ibid.

Solomon Gomes is Senior Political Officer at Darfur Integrated Task Force.

African Renaissance
Vol. 4 No.1 Quarter 1 2007
pp91-99

Due Process and Procurement in the Nigerian Public Sector

Chika N. Oguonu

Abstract:

This article looks at Due Process and Procurement in the Public Sector. The article gives a brief background of Nigeria, a general overview of Due process and Procurement System in Nigerian Public Sector and the major challenges of Due Process Mechanism. It finally draws conclusion and makes recommendations on how best Nigeria can maximize the benefits of effective Procurement System through Due Process Mechanism.

Introduction

Background to the Problem

Nigerian history since independence has been stormy. There was a civil war from 1966 to 1970 and there have been five consecutive military coups. Nigeria is blessed with mineral resources. Agriculture used to dominate the Nigerian economy. "Hence at the eve of political independence in 1960, the proportion of GDP contributed by agriculture (embracing crop cultivation, livestock, fisheries and forestry stood at 67.0 percent, while that of petroleum was only 0.6 percent" (Obinna, 1997, 1). However, with the oil boom of 1970s, agriculture was neglected. This raised the Nigerian level of imported consumption and overdependence of manufacturing sector on imports. Nigerian economy after the oil boom has not been free from problems despite the various attempts from government. Obinna (1997) notes that the launching of the ambitious national development plan (1970-74) and the expedient use of contract awards for execution of national projects helped in breeding social ills in the economy. These include the culture of excessive costs, corrupt management and ill-considered contracts.

From being a middle income country in the 1970s Nigeria has fallen to be amongst the poorest nations in the world. It should be noted that in the 1960s and early 1970s, Nigeria, Malaysia, Indonesia, Taiwan, Singapore and South Korea had similar income per capital, GDP growth rates and under-developed political structure (Ekpo, 2004). However, the Asian

Tigers (Newly industrialized countries (NICs) have actually escaped underdevelopment and poverty. Most people attribute this to the way their economies are being managed. Nigeria has gone through all the phases of business cycle-decline, depression (recession), recovery and boom. Yet none of these booms as Ekpo (2004) noted has resulted in any significant restructuring and transformation of the economy since each boom came and disappeared without being linked to the real sector and none of the benefits associated with the booms was maximized.

Nigeria, especially since the early 80s has been confronted with a magnitude of economic problems. These economic problems, in brief, include stagnant growth, rising inflation, unemployment, food shortage and mounting external debt. Nigeria therefore like most other nations, has been battling with how to achieve its major economic objectives. These objectives include full employment, price stability, economic growth and healthy balance of payments. It has not been easy for Nigeria to realize the above objectives. Some of the factors responsible for this are

1) Poor Performance of the preferred sectors (Agriculture and Manufacturing sectors). These sectors are not doing well because of the following reasons:
a) Unwillingness of investors to invest in our manufacturing sector due to political instability
b) Misplacement of Priorities
c) Shortage of Basic infrastructural amenities and utilities
d) Problems of raw Materials
e) Inherent problems of agriculture in Nigeria

2) Over dependence of Nigerian Economy on a single commodity i.e. oil.
3) Management problems
4) Social problems
5) Inadequate statistical data for policy formulation
6) Inadequate infrastructural amenities
7) Gaps in the judicial and law enforcement agents
8) Lack of effective implementation policy
9) Lack of enabling environment

At the root of all these problems is Corruption. As Obasanjo (2004) rightly observed,
until 1999, Nigeria

... had practically institutionalized corruption as the foundation of governance. Hence institutions of society easily decayed to unprecedented proportions as opportunities were privatized by the powerful. This process was accompanied, as to be expected, by the intimidation of the judiciary, the subversion of due process, the manipulation of existing laws and regulations, the suffocation of civil society, and the containment of democratic values and institutions. Power became nothing but a means of accumulation and subversion as productive initiatives were abandoned for purely administrative and transactional activities. The legitimacy and stability of the state became compromised as citizens began to devise extra-legal and informal ways of survival. All this made room for corruption.

There is therefore an urgent call for Procurement Reforms and enthronement of Due Process in the Nigerian public Sector. In 2001, the Federal Government issued New Policy Guidelines for procurement and award of contracts in Government Ministries/Parastatals (Circular F. 15775 of 27th June, 2001).

Conceptual Clarifications

Due Process implies that governmental activities and businesses can be carried out openly, economically and transparently without favouritism and corruptible tendencies (Ezekwesili, 2004). The essence of this is to ensure that rules and procedures for procurement are made in such a way as to be implementable and enforceable. It is hoped that this Due Process should put an end to "the Business as Usual Syndrome" in Nigeria. Due Process is a mechanism that certifies for public funding only those projects that have passed the test of proper implementation packaging and that adhere stringently to the international competitive bid approach in the award process (Obasanjo, 2003).

There is no gain saying the fact that improved Public Procurement systems would have a beneficial effect on economic condition of the nation. Wittig(1999) views Public Procurement as a business process within a given political system, with distinct considerations of integrity, accountability, national interest and effectiveness. These business operations of government, as controlled by public procurement, usually affect many different elements of society. The procuring entities for instance have needs for material support like roads, hospitals, etc. to help in fulfilling their designated national mission. The business communities of actual or potential suppliers on the other hand need to satisfy government procurement requirement. There are also other interested parties like professional bodies, various agencies, interested public, etc who are all affected or influenced in one way or the other by public procurement.

Due Process and Procurement in the Nigerian Public Sector

Based on wide spread corruption, conducting government business degenerated so much by the year 2000. This was due to the fact that no serious attention was paid to Public Service Rule, Financial Regulations and Ethics and Norms because of selfish reasons. The Federal Government noted the urgent need for transparency in government procedures so as to be able to move the system forward. Hence the Federal Government in 2000 commissioned the World Bank to collaborate with some Private Sector Specialists to study Financial Systems and general procurement-related activities in the country. The essence of this request to the World Bank is to assist Nigerian Government "with a process of enthroning efficiency, accountability, integrity and transparency in Government Procurement and Financial Management Systems" (Ekpenkhio, 2003). It was based on this that the Country Procurement Assessment Report was produced through a participatory review approach from key stake holders including representatives from private sectors and the Federal, State and Local Governments with assistance from international and national consultants. The Country Procurement Assessment Report (CPAR) identified some major weaknesses in the procurement system in Nigeria as follows (Ekpenkhio, 2003):

> 1) That Nigeria lacks a modern law on Public Procurement and Permanent oversight and monitor purchasing entities
> 2) That the finance (Control and Management) Act, 1958, together with Financial Regulations which set basic rules for managing public expenditure have gaps, deficiencies and faulty implementation of existing regulations on procurement (e.g. lack of permanent arrangements for control and surveillance) which create opportunities for bribery and corruption.
> 3) That due to inflation and lack of regular adjustments on the thresholds of the approving limits of the Tender Boards, their authorization were constantly being eroded resulting in abuses, prominent among which is splitting of contracts.
> 4) That there was proliferation of tender boards which were perceived by the private sector as sources of delays and non transparency. In addition, these tender boards appeared to have limited mandates with powers to decide contracts *de facto* resting with the permanent Secretary and the Minister/ Commissioner.
> 5) That Customs systems and procedures were cumbersome and major causes of delay in clearing goods, and hence a source of corruption; and
> 6) That Procurement is often carried out by staff who substantially lack relevant training.

Another major problem to the existing procurement system and guidelines in the country is the difficulty of implementation. The reasons for this as Ezekwesili (2004) pointed out include absence of economic cost/benefit analysis of projects. There is lack of genuine competition and transparency since applicable rules are usually tilted in favour of a predetermined winner. Most projects are not harmonized and are not selected on priority bases. There are gaps between budget and actual releases, which usually result in under funding, delayed competition, price escalating and abandonment. It is based on the above identified weaknesses that The Country Procurement Assessment Report (CPAR) made the following recommendations (Ekpenkhio, 2003):

a) The need for a procurement law based on the United Nations Commission for International Trade Model (UNCITRAL).
b) The need to establish a Public Procurement Commission (PPC) to serve as the regulatory and oversight body on Public Sector Procurements
c) The revision of key areas of the financial regulations to make them more transparent;
d) The streamlining of Tender Boards and the strengthening of their functional authority, including powers to award contracts.
e) A critical need to rebuild procurement and financial management capacity in the public sector; and
f) a comprehensive review of the businesses related to export, import and transit regulations, procedures and practices.

It should be noted that the government "accepted The Country Procurement Assessment Report (CPAR) report in its entirety with the exception of the Registration of Contractors and the involvement of Political Office holders such as Ministers/Commissioners in the award of contracts in excess of fifty million Naira which the report was against" (Ekpenkhio, 2003)

The Obasanjo administration decided to stop the "Business as Usual Syndrome" by establishing the Budget Monitoring and Price Intelligence Unit (BMPIU) in the Presidency. By so doing, the government aimed at formulating and implementing appropriate policies on procurement and contract awards. The Budget Monitoring and Price Intelligence Unit (BMPIU) serves as a "vanguard of ensuring fiscal transparency, strict compliance with Federal Government guidelines on Due Process Certification as it concerns budgeting for and procurement of facilities/services/contracts at appropriate costs"(Ezekwesili, 2005). The Budget Monitoring and Price Intelligence Unit (BMPIU), which also addresses the development and operation of procurement of services for Federal Government and its agencies, has the following objectives (Ezekwesili, 2005):

1) To harmonize existing government policies/practices and update same on public procurement.
2) To determine whether or not Due Process has been observed in the procurement of services and contracts through the initiation and execution of such projects.
3) To introduce more probity, accountability and transparency into the procurement process.
4) To establish and update pricing standards and benchmarks for all supplies to government
5) To monitor the implementation of projects during execution with a view to providing information on performance, output, compliance with specifications and targets (cost, quality and time).

6) To ensure that only projects which have been budgeted for are admitted for execution.

7) To ensure that Budget spending is based on authentic reasonable and fair costing.

The mission of The Budget Monitoring and Price Intelligence Unit (BMPIU) is "To use Due Process Mechanism to establish Transparent, Competitive and Fair Procurement System, which is integrity-driven, encourages spending within budget and ensures speedy delivery of projects, while achieving value for money without sacrificing quality and standards for the Federal government of Nigeria." For realization of The Budget Monitoring and Price Intelligence Unit (BMPIU) objectives, the government put in place the regulatory functions for regulating standards including the enforcement of harmonized bidding and tender documents, certification functions for certifying federal-wide procurements in categories of Resident Due Process Team certification (projects with a threshold of between N1.0 million and N50 million) and Full Due Process Certification (Projects above N50 million at various stages), Monitoring functions to supervise the implementation of established procurement policies and training and advisory functions to co-ordinate relevant training programmes (Ezekwesili, 2005). The documents to be forwarded to The Budget Monitoring and Price Intelligence Unit (BMPIU) as requirements for Due Process Review as outlined by Ezekwesili include:

1)The Project Policy file
2) Evidence of Advertisement as appropriate
3)Tender Returns
4)Tender Evaluation Report
5) Contract Award Letter and Agreement
6) Original Contract Bills of Quantities (if any)
7) Contract Drawings (if any)
8) Other Contract Documents
9) Financial Summary and Statements
10) Progress Reports
11) Variation Requests and Variation Orders arising
12) Interim Valuation and Certificates.

Due Process mechanism has made reasonable progress in Nigeria. Within two years of its implementation, progress has been made especially in the promotion of fair play and competition. A lot of savings have been made especially in the area of reduction to contract sums, in some cases to the tune of $500 million(Obasanjo, 2003). Obasanjo (2003) also stated that "the Due Process Mechanism has saved Nigeria over N102 billion in two years arising from various federal government's over-bloated contracts". Ezekwesili, (2003) also disclosed that her office "saved N672.4 million (an equivalent of 4.1 million Euros) from a single project by the Ministry of

Health meant to procure and supply equipment to tertiary health institutions". Various contracts awarded with spending units that failed to comply with laid down competitive bid parameters have been cancelled. Inflation of contract has also reduced to a reasonable extent. There is also a general awareness of anti corruption mechanism put in place by Government..

However there are some problems which The Budget Monitoring and Price Intelligence Unit (BMPIU) faces. These problems, as highlighted by Ezekwesili, include the ignorance and unwillingness of some officials to comply with the provisions of the circulars. Again, at the initiation of some projects there is inadequate project definition and scope definition. Professionals are also not involved in some project packaging and supervision. In other cases there is improper in-house pricing arising out of inadequate continuous professional development. Again, there is in some cases insufficient or inadequate documentation, accompanying requests for certification and delays in responding to issues raised in the draft Due Process Review Report.

Conclusion and recommendations

It should be noted that Due Process and Procurement reforms produced some useful dividends. It resulted in a more transparent, efficient and effective procurement system which creates equal access to bidders of public sector contracts. It has led to an increase in Government revenue base by minimizing avenues of wastages and leakages in the economy through efficient management of government resources. It has made it possible for contractors and suppliers to have a fair hearing when aggrieved through filing their protests to a statutory contract appeal Board (Ekpenkhio, 2003). However Ekpenkhio suggested that to fully maximize the benefits of procurement reforms, there is need to develop a new cadre of professional procurement officers and contracting officers in the public service for the implementation of procurement reforms. He also argued that it would be necessary to work out an appropriate scheme of service to be adopted by all the tiers of government for procurement and contracting officers. Capacity building and training (at home and abroad) workshops, seminars, and courses for new cadre of Procurement and Contracting Officers and all those involved in procurement awards should be organized. It is also necessary to restructure ministries to create cadres of procurement officers and contracting officers in the public service so as to make for uniform implementation and easy monitoring of the procurement reforms. There is equally the need to build consensus among the three tiers of government in order to promote the smooth implementation of the procurement reforms by a law which is binding on all the tiers of government.

Finally, it should be emphasized that for effective Procurement System through Due Process, a lot still needs to be done. There is for instance a need for institutionalizing, internalizing and building ownership for the multitude of reforms within the public sector so as to ensure that it sustains the changes in the anti-corruption campaign. Some people feel that our legislators are found wanting in this area. It is necessary that legislators should play a leading role in enthroning the principles of openness, accountability, probity and transparency. They must behave in such a way that they are seen and perceived by the public as the epitome of integrity. To be able to gain such respect, it is necessary that the legislative bodies and their members reflect the highest corporate and personal standards of ethics and integrity. On the part of the judiciary too, a lot is still desired from them especially as regards building confidence for its vital role in the sanctioning of corrupt conducts. The public perceives the judiciary as still battling with corruption, which makes the prosecution and the judicial process less effective. Another criticism is levelled on Anti-Corruption Commission for its inability, in most instances, to successfully prosecute and sentence any high level public official for corruption. The Commission however has always blamed this on the failure of the judicial process which usually does not respond speedily and appropriately to the quest for effective sanctioning of corrupt acts (Obasanjo, 2003). These trends should stop for dividends of Due Process to be realized.

The importance of Due Process Mechanism can not be overemphasized. It is a framework for implementation and it is committed to tackling corruption, promoting transparency and accountability in Nigeria polity.

Refrences

Obasanjo O. (2003) "Nigeria: From Pond of Corruption to Island of Integrity" Lecture Delivered at the 10th Anniversary Celebration of Transparency InternationalBerlin.

Obasanjo O. (2004) "Due Process Saves Nigeria N102 bn" *This Day,* Nigeria.

Ekpenkhio S.A. (2003) "Public Sector Procurement Reforms: The Nigerian Experience"A paper presented to the Government of the Federation at the Regional Workshop On Procurement Reforms and Transparency in Government Procurement for Anglophone African Countries in Tanzania.

Ekpo A.H. (2004) "The Nigerian Economy Under a New Democratic Experience: The

Charles Soludo Effect" A paper presented at The Convocation Ceremony at University of Nigeria, Nsukka.

Ezekwesili O (2005) "Due Process Mechanism and Digital Opportunities" Paper presented to the University Community at Princess

Alexandria Auditorium, University o fNigeria, Nsukka.

International Monetary Fund (2005) "Nigeria and IMF: 2005 Article IV Consultation Concluding Statement"

Obinna O.E. (1997) "Economic Revival and Sustainance in Nigeria: What Hope for Fourth Republic?" Paper presented at the Seminar on Vision and Mission of Governance and Development in Nigeria in Fourth Republic, organized by Division of General Studies, University of Nigeria, Nsukka.

Wittig W.A. (1999) "Building Value Through Public Procurement: A Focus on Africa"9th International Anti-Corruption Conference, Durban, South Africa.

Dr Chika N. Oguonu is at the Univesity of Nigeria, Nsukka

African Renaissance
Vol. 4 No.1 Quarter 1 2007
pp101-107

Post-Colonial Africa and Post-War Japan:
Convergence and Divergence

Seifudein Adem

Edmond Burke once wrote that it is by imitation, far more than by precept, that we learn everything. With a view to making informed judgment about whether or not Africa should and could imitate Japan, this essay briefly reviews competing theories about Japan's success in modernization and Africa's failure to modernize, contrasts the divergent approaches to economic and political modernization pursued by each, and raises a question about the convergence between the collective cultural identities of the two.

Japan's successful modernization

A plethora of theories have sought to explain why Japan succeeded, ranging from, on the one hand, that Japan succeeded because it was completely westernized to, on the other hand, the nation succeeded because the nation clung to its core values and traditions. Other perspectives fall somewhere in between the two positions. On the whole these perspectives may be classified into three ideal types. Most dominant in the period prior to the Second World War was the externally-oriented school which maintained that Japan succeeded because it abandoned its culture. According to this school Japan borrowed from the West not just scientific techniques but also the values and institutions which support them and therefore Japan's modernization was nothing less than Westernization. Natsume Soseki is perhaps one of the more renowned Meiji Japan intellectuals who had held this type of view.

Japan succeeded because it remained loyal to its culture, claimed the internally-oriented school. It was Japan's culture which provided the foundations for sustained economic growth and industrialization. This school not only rejected the Euro-centric notion that non-Western societies cannot modernize without substantial input from the West but argued that it was, in fact, Japan's pre-capitalistic, and even feudal culture that prepared the necessary condition for Japan's modernization. This view was most fashionable in the postwar period. Masao Maruyama's and Akio

Morita's views, among others, are representative of this school. Then comes the hybrid theory which attributed the success of Japan to a creative synthesis of "the Japanese spirit and the Western techniques". This approach has persisted across different phases of the modernization of Japan, recruiting in the process many articulate proponents, the most well-known of whom is the great Japanese educator Yukichi Fukuzawa.

Africa's unsuccessful modernization

Why did Africa fail to modernize? Using the same classificatory schema used in the case of Japan, the explanations about Africa's failure to modernize can be categorized into externally-oriented, internally-oriented and hybrid. Theories such as "Europe underdeveloped Africa" or, in general, "the industrialized world underdeveloped Africa" are externally-oriented theories. World systems theorists, dependentistas and Neo-Marxists have sometimes advanced ideas reflective of this approach. The best known scholar belonging to this school is, perhaps, Walter Rodney, the author of *How Europe Underdeveloped Africa*. On the other hand, theories which attribute Africa's underdevelopment to the alleged fact, as it is sometimes put bluntly, that "Africans are lazy" or that "African societies are low-trust societies" belong to the group of internally-oriented explanations of underdevelopment. It must be also pointed out that these theories are, more often than not, based on extrapolation of findings outside Africa. Influential scholars such as Samuel Huntington and Francis Fukuyama espouse views which are in tune with this perspective. Apparently, the perspective which is becoming increasingly popular in recent years among many Africanists and some policy-makers is that which sees the combination of internal and external factors as the primary culprits.

Economic modernization, culture and ideology

In general Japan's response to challenges of modernization was more culturally-mediated than that of post-colonial Africa where ideology seemed to have played a greater part.

Let me briefly illustrate what I mean, starting with the place of modification and authenticity. The Japanese modified imported ideas and institutions, ranging from Confucianism to capitalism, and adapted them to local conditions without much concern about whether the end product had or did not have close resemblance to the original. In other words the principle of creative imitation, itself deeply rooted in their culture, guided the Japanese endeavor.

Unlike the Japanese, Africans did not have a major say in the process of selecting which ideas and institutions to import. Whatever new ideas came from abroad, they were either imposed from above/outside or the choice was merely a result of the conspiracy of circumstances. And yet Africa's post-colonial modernizers tried to stick to the script of a foreign idea as much as possible, believing vacillating between one system of ideas and another, or blending different systems, was a sign of indetermination. The guiding force behind Africa's pursuit of foreign ideas thus seemed to be ideological authenticity even as the ultimate goal was bound up with social purpose. This was again in contrast to the Japanese approach which favored not only the shifting of gears from one system to another but the blending of different systems too.

We should also bear in mind, however, that the choices which were available to Japan were not as disharmonious as the ones with which post-colonial Africa was confronted. Japan had the luxury of choosing between the American model and the British, or the French and the Prussian, etc., and these models were not always mutually exclusive to the same degree for instance as between liberal-capitalism and Marxism-Leninism.

A related factor to the Japanese proclivity to modify which also contributed to their success in economic modernization is flexibility—the versatility to change as circumstances require. Japanese culture allows considerable degree of flexibility. The general tendency in contemporary Africa has not been very favorable for flexibility; but a great potential seems to exist in Africa too for developing this cultural resource. So long as African cultures attach greater significance to experience than ideology, which they do as I shall argue shortly, it is plausible to argue that African cultures are not incompatible with the principle of flexible accommodation. That Africa's cultural capital hasn't been fully utilized doesn't mean that the potential is not there. Empirical studies strongly suggest that cultural resources could be revitalized for utilization even centuries after they were lying dormant.

And as far as continuity and change are concerned, Japan's modernizers never sought a radical transformation of their culture in order to modernize. They saw to it that if there was a change, it was only incremental, often with a sort of link between the old and the new. They never doubted that one could be modern and traditional at the same time. On the other hand, Africa's abortive modernization efforts were based on a host of "new" foreign ideas, and Africa's post-independence modernizers often sought to transform traditional culture in a fundamental way, with little or no attempt to incorporate the modern into the traditional, or vice versa. In the end, the old was badly dismantled, and the new was not also in place. The effort itself was never ill-intended of course, but the outcome almost always turned out to be disappointing. The Japanese mobilized their energy and resources to build a new, modern society when they were engaged in the modernization effort; they did not labor as much to abolish age-old practices, or completely cut themselves off from the past. In short Japan's experience in economic modernization bears out that it is useful to be flexible, it is crucial to link traditional values to modern ideas, and it is imperative to rely on one's own cultural resources.

Japan's political experience and Africa's challenges

Let me now turn attention to comparative politics in post-colonial Africa and post-Cold War Japan. The reason why pos-colonial Africa is chosen is obvious; but how about post-Cold War Japan? Japanese political scientists call the 1990s "the years of trial". In that decade Japan changed its governments nine times. Despite such a high frequency of change, political transitions were nevertheless peaceful. And it was this simple observation which leads one to ask the following questions. Why is political change in Japan peaceful while in Africa it is less so? Does culture play a part? At least four factors can be identified in this context.

Firstly politics is not perceived in Japan as a-zero-sum game, certainly not to the same extent as elsewhere, including in Africa. In fact one Japanese political scientist has argued that the effectiveness of a politician should be judged by the extent to which he/she could successfully make compromises between conflicting positions. One way of arriving at this type of compromise is by ensuring a loser of today could be a winner of tomorrow. As I elaborate shortly, the Japanese have succeeded in doing just that.

In Africa, more often than not, you lose a political contest, a contest which is sometimes bloody and violent, then that marks the end of your political career, but it could also even mean physical extermination or long-term imprisonment. In much of Africa the unwritten rule of the game seems to be if you are in a political contest, you have two choices: either to win and exterminate your opponents or to lose and be exterminated. This is where contemporary Japanese political system is at variance with its African counterpart.

Secondly there is political recycling. By political recycling I mean public utilization of senior statesmen who had been out of service for one reason or another. A net effect of political recycling is the institutionalization of a multiple-sum game of politics, or its perception as such.

The idea of political recycling fosters the desire among political contestants not only to be good losers but also gracious winners. In this dynamics also lie what Robert Axelrod in his book, *The Evolution of Cooperation*, had called a condition of robust cooperation among political actors because of the large shadow of the future which guarantees that another encounter between same political actors is almost inevitable and that defection under the circumstances becomes unprofitable strategy. In Africa the concept of political recycling is virtually unknown. If a leader captures political power he realizes that that is his only chance and should cling to it by all means.

A most enabling factor to the vibrancy and healthy functioning of political recycling in Japan is the transient nature of hierarchy. Even though the Japanese tend to view things hierarchically, real or imagined, political hierarchy is also seen as transient. It does not therefore bother Keiichi Miyazawa, the former prime minister of Japan, to work as a Finance Minister two years after stepping down as prime minister. The same is true about former Prime Minister Hashimoto and many other ex-prime-ministers and senior politicians. In general, in Africa, with one or two exceptions, no example springs to mind of a leader who had been on the helms of power, had lost office and came back to re-assume a top position in the national government, let alone serve in a position lower than one he had held previously.

Thirdly, the win-win perspective such as the above also stems from, and results in the distinct nature of conflict resolution in Japan. Japan's political culture, on balance, favors good rather than right if, for the sake of argument, we disregard the fact that what is good and what is right are themselves culturally contingent. In the Japanese system of thought, morality usually means establishing harmony, rather than justice; in other words, it is a system that encourages accommodation between the winner and the loser.

The nature of conflict resolution in Africa is, on the whole, more clear-cut, vindicating one side and criminalizing the other, elevating one to the status of a victor and the other becoming vanquished. The Japanese thus follow, in other words, the "victor without vanquished" formula in contrast to the "crime and punishment" method used in Africa. In Africa's conflict resolution mechanism it is as if political contestants are unable to grasp they had won unless their opponents were humiliatingly defeated, and even crushed—both metaphorically and literally.

The fourth factor pertains to the social identity of the principal political actors. Even a cursory look at the professional background of post-Second World War Japanese prime ministers reveals that they come from diverse social background. What they all have in common is a non-military background. Not only the prime ministers, but also all the key players in the Japanese national politics are professionals from areas other than the military. In fact, the overwhelming majority of Japanese prime ministers and other senior politicians had acquired at one time or another professional training or experience in an area pertaining to economics. And virtually all of them had gone to a handful of select elite universities in the country.

Comparatively, the situation in many African countries is quite different. In most cases, those who occupy the highest office are the powerful; and those who are powerful have for the most part a military background, either as former leaders of liberation movements, or as defense ministers or senior officers in the ministry. The identity as well as background of these individuals, it seems, also conditions them to perceive politics as a zero-sum game.

Japans' political system, like its economic system, is deeply rooted in its culture. This is good news for Africa because it suggests that Africa too could draw upon its own culture in devising a most suitable system of governance.

Africa and Japan: overlapping cultural identities?

Africa and Japan are closer culturally than it is generally recognized. And yet the Japanese are the last to admit their culture has shared elements with African cultures; some would even regard such a notion as bordering on blasphemy. At least three possible reasons have relevance to the explanation of the Japanese resistance to any form of cultural affinity with Africa.

The first stems from the fact that such a view clashes with the Japanese belief that they are special people. The Japanese believe—and they want others to believe—that they are a chosen people. Another source of resistance is the natural tendency of humans to distance themselves from their less successful fellow beings. Part of the explanation has also to do with the prevalence of ignorance about Africa in Japan, and the absence of incentives to rectify it. The latter is in turn a function of history, economics, politics and geography.

In any case the distinguished Africanist Ali Mazrui has characterized the elder and sage traditions, among others, as two of the major elements in the socio-cultural ideologies of African political thought. I limit my brief discussion here to the corresponding traditions in Japan, their expressions and how they are utilized for the betterment of the society.

It is a well-known fact that the Japanese place heavy premium on age. There are even some observers who characterize the Japanese political system as being closer to a gerontocracy than it is to democracy. One important feature of this tradition is the maximum value attached to experience rather than ideology. The principle of seniority through which party and government leaders are elected to office is one practical manifestation. With a handful of exceptions all of the post-War prime ministers of Japan were senior both in age and experience in comparison to the next in line.

Another indication of the greater value attached to age and experience pertains to the utilization of the expertise of leaders of the preceding governments even after they are displaced by new ones, what I have called political recycling above. Greatly stabilizing the system, the elder tradition serves in this way as a basis for political continuity.

The sage tradition, on the other hand, is connected to that element of Japanese political thought which conceptualizes political leadership as the task of the wise. This tradition also supplements the elder tradition rather than undermining it. The wise is usually one with a wealth of experience who, in most cases, would also be relatively advanced in age. Although

106

age, too, factors in the sage tradition, it is not the decisive one. What seems to be more important in the sage tradition is the acquisition of an acceptable level of formal education preferably in one of the elite institutions of higher education in the country, a situation which further introduces important dimension of shared experience among the key political actors.

Conclusion

In comparing Japan and Africa, it must be remembered that an important factor in the modernization of Japan was also the fact that Japan was never colonized—a fate which enabled it to escape the kind of negative consequences colonialism brought to Africa, including the disruption of the consolidation of Africa's own traditional institutions. That Japan is a mono-ethnic nation in contrast to the multi-ethnic states of post-colonial Africa was another consequential factor in Africa's modernization effort.

A comparative study of Africa and Japan seems to suggest (and even support) three broad but inter-related generalizations about challenges of modernizations. As a rule, the problems which confront all societies at different stages are limited in scope and they boil down to the question of how to improve the human condition. And secondly, the range of solutions is also of finite variability even though the collective actions and reactions of all societies to internal and external stimuli are always mediated by particular set of beliefs, assumptions and worldviews. This is the issue of finite solutions. The potential for solving the common challenges exists in all cultures in a variety of forms. Every culture, every society has the potential for successfully tackling the challenges of modernization, but there is no universal model of doing so. In other words the potential for overcoming the challenges of modernization is universal but the approach for doing so is not.

As a product of the "triple heritage", it must be underscored, Africa's cultural dispositions present no exception in regard to the above generalizations in spite of the multitude of challenges the continent faces today. And this should give us good reason to be optimistic about the prospect of African renaissance.

African Renaissance
Vol. 4 No.1 Quarter 1 2007
pp108-113

The West And Michael Peel's Africa

Uche Nworah

Section One: Still On Western Media Imperialism

The developing world, Africa in particular, has always argued against the imbalances and injustices in the coverage of their affairs by the western media. Such coverage is not only paternalistic but often grossly unfair, and serves only to sustain the imperialistic interests of the developed world. Such unbalanced, negative and biased reporting is bound to continue because of the concentration of global media networks and resources in the West.

It is indeed sad that 26 years after the UNESCO sponsored McBride Commission and Report, the recommendations are yet to be fully implemented; the most significant of which is the suggestion for 'the progressive implementation of national and international measures that will foster the setting up of a new world information and communication order'.

If anything, the information divide between the developed and developing countries has widened even further, especially in this digital age which is being driven by globalization and technology. Africa and the rest of the developing world have found themselves again lagging behind the west.

However, a little goodwill and responsibility on the part of the western media is really needed at this time to prevent the continued psychological scares and damages, leading sometimes to feelings of inferiority complex on the part of the African as a result of continued sensationalisation and criminalisation of everything African.

Not all Africans are criminals, rapists and savages. Also, there are many good things about Africa. Not all Africans live in slums; neither do they all scavenge rubbish heaps for food. Africa has also produced intellectuals and academics that can stand their own in the western world. Agreed the continent still faces peculiar challenges, but so does the rest of the developed world.

A situation where little efforts on the part of African governments and their people to take control of their destiny are either unreported, misreported, under-reported or acknowledged with cynicism by the western media is unacceptable, and does not indicate respect for the continent, neither does it reflect the ideals of partnership, a concept that Western leaders have been touting lately.

But why do the western media still thrive on a culture of negative and biased reporting of Africa and her people? It could be as a result of the need to improve ratings, which can only be achieved by satisfying the mundane voyeuristic tastes and expectations of the western media audience, whose colonial views of Africa as the backward and dark continent must be reinforced and sustained. It could also be as a result of the immoral culture and acceptance by the western media that 'bad news sells', and hence news about hunger in Sudan depicting dying children, or about savagery in Rwanda must be sought and reported by all means, even if at the sacrifice and expense of the developmental needs of the African, as well as their national interests.

Again, the McBride Report was published at a time when global media concentration was in the hands of national governments and their agencies, the understanding must have been that these governments would prevail on the media networks through directed policies to encourage a new world information and communication order. Because the report is advisory in nature and relied on goodwill from the stakeholders without any legislative powers to enforce sanctions, it had remained merely what it is – a report and doesn't seem to have made much impact, despite the efforts by Africans to set up the Pan African News Agency (PANA), billed as the voice of Africa to the world and representing the African perspective, not much could be said to have been achieved and it has been business as usual ever since.

Finally, the greater concentration of global media networks in the west, i.e. CNN, BBC, FOX, Reuters, AFP etc, coupled with the availability of material and human resources have meant that western media are able to come up first with the news, as against African media networks such as NTA, SABC, PANA, NAN, AIT etc who are still bogged by dearth of resources, and therefore can not cope in the global news race, thus limiting their chances of covering the African continent positively. It is such that Africans have had to rely on the western media for news coverage of events happenings right under their noses, or in their back yards. The western media are able to deploy resources even to the remotest regions, they can afford to since they have both the resources and personnel. Not the same can be said of African media networks.

Africans may also be guilty of helping to perpetuate this neo-colonialism, western journalists and writers and their chauvinistic views are culled, easily celebrated and given media spaces in African media channels, not minding that the situation reversed becomes like the proverbial camel passing through the eye of the needle for African writers and journalists to be published in the western media, with the exception of a few African writers and journalists who maintain the western status quo, unwilling to rock the boat.

Few incidents reported recently in the United Kingdom (UK) media drives home this point. The Tony Blair government has been embroiled in a battle for political survival since their battering at the last local government elections in May 2006.

The Blair government is looking for sacrificial lambs every where to make up for the government's ineptitude in certain areas, and also to satisfy the interests of the media. It appears that they have zeroed in on Africans and other immigrants in the UK. The British media have now successfully created the impression in the minds of the ever increasing nationalistic UK citizens, that immigrants are evil and criminal. Matters were also not helped by the fact that <u>over a thousand dangerous criminals</u> were mistakenly released, some of whom allegedly were supposed to be deported but weren't as a result of a Home Office error.

Newspapers such as the Evening Standard went to town recently with a screaming headline announcing that <u>5 Nigerian illegal immigrants</u> were caught working in the home office. A further analysis actually showed that the immigrants in question worked as cleaners under contract by another firm.

Such biased headlines actually undermine the importance of immigrants in most western economies. Considering the low wages paid to workers in the cleaning and related sectors, it remains to be seen if citizens of these countries would agree to work such menial jobs at the ludicrous wages the immigrants are paid for their services.

It appears Nigeria now represents everything evil in eyes of the western media as they are quick to give front page coverage with screaming headlines to matters concerning the country. Take the case of <u>Dr Richard Akinrolabu,</u> a senior house officer at St Richard's Hospital, Chichester who was accused by his lover and colleague of attempting to carry out illegal abortion procedures on her. The doctor was named and shamed in front page headlines which were written along the lines of 'Nigerian Doctor ...' His accuser, the white woman did not suffer the same fate. In the end, the case was thrown out but not after the huge embarrassment to the doctor and his fellow country men. You would expect the media to also accord the not-guilty verdict the same headlines and coverage but they did not.

Another example of western media misreporting of Africa and Africans could be seen in the case of <u>Guy Koma,</u> who mistakenly became an interview guest on the BBC News 24 programme. Due to a scheduling mix-up, Mr Koma who had gone to the BBC centre for a job interview was mistaken for the scheduled guest (Guy Kewney) but still managed to 'talk' his way through the session although he had no clue of the interview theme. The UK media revelled in the story because of its human interest angle but wrongly identified Mr Koma as a taxi driver. Not that there is anything wrong with being a taxi driver but the media's judgment could only have been influenced by their age-old prejudices as to the type of jobs

African immigrants do. It has since been confirmed that Mr Koma was actually attending a job interview in the IT department of BBC at the time of the mix-up. There were no follow-up reports on whether he got the job, not that Mr Koma would mind anyway because he has since signed a lucrative movie deal with an American production company over the incident, and is billed to play himself in the movie.

Section Two: Michael Peel's Africa

Perhaps Africa's and indeed Nigeria's biggest enemy with regards to negative and biased reporting is Michael Peel, I have indeed tried to contain myself and to be patient with this voyeur cum journalist but I can not hold myself anymore. Not after his last <u>damning report</u> and one-sided take on fraud and scams purportedly emanating out of Nigeria which he claims costs the United Kingdom billions annually.

As we say in Nigeria, enough is enough. How long should we stand by and watch this fellow dehumanise Africans and indeed Nigerians with his negative take on the African continent? This past week, most of the United Kingdom newspapers have been awash with Mr Peel's story, conversations on tubes and buses and in offices have been ignited once again with the story of Nigerians and their financial invention – the 419 scam. But this is not all that Nigerians are good at; unfortunately it is the only one that Michael Peel chose to tell the world.

For people like me who speak the English language flavoured with a thick Nigerian accent, and who bear flag-waving African names, there is no escaping the scorn, 'sympathies' and jeers. As the West African correspondent of the Financial Times Newspaper, Michael Peel has never found anything good and positive in the whole sub-region worth reporting, his reports are usually couched in cynicism, threads of decay, death and backwardness knit them together, just like the news reports of his fellow western media journalists stationed in Africa whose only mandate is to report the bad and ugly. For Michael Peel and his associates, there is nothing good coming out of Africa; Africa is still a dark continent and its people savages and criminals.

I often wonder, when they go to bed at night, do they calmly shut their eyes with the satisfaction that they have done their best through their many warped and negative reports to improve the lives of the Africans whom they constantly denigrate, or does the thought that they may be contributing to Africa's backwardness linger somewhere on their minds?

As an associate fellow of <u>Chatham House,</u> does Michael Peel not realise that the documents he authors and which are endorsed by Chatham House in a way influences policies including the decisions taken by governments and global investors concerning Africa, and that such parochial take on issues is at cross purposes with Africa, and indeed Nigeria's march towards national re-birth, and its current drive to attract foreign direct investments (FDIs)?

Where has the journalistic objectivity he learnt in journalism school gone to? In telling his readers how much the United Kingdom loses annually to fraud emanating from Nigeria, he conveniently ignored the fact that his fellow citizens (the 'innocent' victims) are also co-perpetrators in the crime, and that their 'misfortune' only came about because of their greed and immoral inclination to rape Africa and rob it of its resources. A disposition that dates centuries and continues to be witnessed in Africa's many mines and oil wells.

So who is smiling last now? The poor Africans that he so much detests and derides constantly, subjecting them to constant ridicule in the western media, and elevating them to favourite dinner table topics, and ballroom party conversations in Westminster through his negative reports, or is it the greedy white men and women who planned to reap where they did not sow and got done in the process?

Maybe Michael Peel should take a cue from <u>John Simpson</u>, BBC's former Africa correspondent and world affairs editor who reports Africa just like a partner in Africa's progress and development should; praising and critiquing it when necessary while at the same time savouring, celebrating and immersing himself in the culture of the people; their food, music, art, and lifestyle. In one of Mr Simpson's many introspective essays published sometime in 2000, in an edition of *High Life*, the British Airways in-flight magazine; John Simpson wrote what I consider to be one of the most beautiful articles about Nigeria ever written by a non-Nigerian. In the said article, he bared his soul while declaring his love for a country that he said was probably one of the best countries in the world to live in despite the odds and challenges. Surely there are things Mr Simpson must have seen or experienced to have made him arrive at such a conclusion. Such an endorsement coming from a widely travelled man and writer obviously beats the many battering at the keyboards of the Michael Peels of this world who may have overstayed their welcome, and should now be thinking of packing their bags and leaving the beautiful continent; the land of the great rivers and the rising sun.

I guess it is only Michael Peel that can produce the statistical formula he used to arrive at the alleged amount of money the United Kingdom loses annually to Nigerian fraudsters, if his billion pounds calculations were true, would there have still been a need for Nigeria and the rest of Africa to be asking for debt cancellation? Would such gigantic proceeds of crime not have been visible on the ground? Would all the roads and pavements in Nigeria not be tarred and paved with gold, and would the economy of the United Kingdom not have seriously felt the impact of such illegal capital flights moving out of the economy to Nigeria?

Michael Peel should please get another vocation and leave Nigeria and Nigerians alone. Scare mongering is hardly what the world needs at this stage, particularly the United Kingdom which currently grapples with a myriad of issues including large scale corporate fraud (post – Enron, Andersen, WorldCom, Tyco etc), organized crime, poverty, anti-social behaviours, teenage pregnancy, threat of terrorism and rising unemployment etc. If he is so much concerned, he should be trawling the studios of the BBC, ITV, Channels 4 and 5 as well as Sky exhorting his people and advising them not to give away their 'billions of pounds' to Nigerians.

Africans and their governments share part of the blame for not fighting their own battles themselves. They have repeatedly failed to invest in their own media systems and infrastructures with which to tell their own stories. It may be along this line though that the Nigerian government-owned Nigerian Television Authority (NTA) recently started broadcasting internationally. Worthy of note also is the reported plans by Nigeria's News Agency of Nigeria (NAN) to begin a 24-hour transmission from January 2007, just like other global news wires. These are all positive moves which if sustained in the longer term would give Nigeria a voice on the global arena, in addition to the little efforts of privately owned terrestrial channels such as Africa Independent Television (AIT), Bright Entertainment Network (BEN) Television, and OBE etc.

The attempt by Mr Peel to palm off his *guestimates* as research in order to support his position and those of his paymasters is indeed appalling; if only he was sincere, a casual probe would have told him that most of the scam emails do not originate from Nigeria, agreed some unscrupulous Nigerians may have popularised the scams but other citizens of the world including citizens of the United Kingdom have since perfected it. Mr Peel can not argue for sure that the daily 'Euro Millions Prize Monies' and such similar scam emails which bombard our email boxes daily all originate from Nigeria, or does he not watch the BBC Watchdog programme? How many Nigerians have been featured in that programme? Are the usual suspects not his fellow countrymen and women who get caught in the act while attempting to fleece other law abiding citizens including pensioners of their hard earned money?

The age-old reliance by African countries on western media such as the BBC, Financial Times, CNN, VOA etc for information has not really done Africa much good. The time has come for Africa and Africans to start telling their own stories, and to commit Michael Peel and his co-travellers who feast on Africa's misfortunes, and are always quick to condemn, judge, blame and criminalise the good people of Africa with their myopic reports to the rubbish bins of history.

Uche Nworah, a freelance writer and lecturer, is the author of the book; *The Long Harmattan Season,* which is available from Amazon.com and iUniverse.com.

African Renaissance
Vol. 4 No.1 Quarter 1 2007
pp114-116

ALI A. MAZRUI: LIVING LEGEND AWARD, 2007:
Acceptance Speech

Speech accepting the Living Legend Award, bestowed on Ali A. Mazrui by the African Communications Agency and the Economic Commission of West African States [ECOWAS] at the 2007 Africa's International Media Summit [AIMS 2007], Abuja, Nigeria, February 13, 2007. Previous Living Legend Honorees include Nelson Mandela, Kofi Annan, Dudley Thompson and Wole Soyinka.

I am truly both honoured and humbled to be recognized as a Living Legend at this AIMS Summit, under the auspices of the Economic Organization of West African States (ECOWAS) and the African Communications Agency.

When one is honoured in this way, there are three factors which make the occasion special to the honouree. One factor is who is making the presentation. In my case, I ask the question: Who today is saluting my contributions to this world of ours? The second factor important to the honouree is: For what am I being recognized today? The third factor significant to the honouree is: Who else is being honoured alongside me? What is the company I am keeping? To what galaxy do I belong?

Prof Ali Mazrui

Before I answer those questions, let me share an anecdote. A few years ago a South African university invited me to receive an honorary doctorate at the same ceremony which was also conferring such a degree on Nelson Mandela. I was, of course, impressed by the university which was honouring me. I was flattered by the tribute to my scholarship, the recognition of my services to Africa. And I felt really good that I was going to be honoured at the same ceremony as Nelson Mandela.

But did I really belong to the same galaxy as Nelson Mandela? I was soon disabused of that fantasy. Nelson Mandela indicated that he would only be able to accept the doctorate if the ceremony was conducted in his village in South Africa. And so instead of the apocryphal Muhammad going to the mountain, the mountain went to Muhammad! The university in question packed its bags, gowns, microphones, hundreds of chairs and dozens of tables -- and packed its buses with students, professors and administrators to go to Nelson Mandela's village. The ceremony was held on the grounds of Mandela's village residence.

My own graduation was held the following day on the campus of that university. Although Ngugi wa Thion'go, the novelist, and I were deeply flattered by the honorary doctorates we received that day, we both also recognized that we were not in the same league as Nelson Mandela. We did not belong to the same galaxy as him. By no stretch of the imagination could we have summoned the apocryphal mountain of the occasion to follow Muhammad to our village.

At the time of recording this acceptance of the Living Legends Award, which is to be conferred on me in Abuja on February 13, 2007, I do not have the list of the other honourees. But I do know that the legendary boxer, sportsman and humanitarian, Muhammad Ali, will be among those being saluted.

As it happens, he is the only sportsman whose autographed and framed photograph hangs in my sitting room in Binghamton, New York. Of course, I do not belong to Muhammad Ali's galaxy either, but at least my own children regard me as the second most famous <u>Black Ali</u> after Muhammad Ali! I am a mere Ali Mazrui.

What is Muhammad Ali's photograph doing in my sitting room? Because he and I once joined forces to raise money for Somalia which was then suffering from famine. At a fundraising banquet in Philadelphia, I was the main speaker and Muhammad Ali was the great presence. That evening and the next day the boxer and I spent many hours together.

On one occasion, when we stood together near Philadelphia's railway station, passers-by recognized Muhammad Ali instantly. But since I was standing by Ali's side, the pedestrians assumed that I was either Muhammad Ali's secretary or his aging body-guard! So those passers-by who wanted Ali's autograph or wanted to shake his hand first came to me for permission. Muhammad Ali authorized me to be the go-between! Autograph-hunters surrounded me -- not asking for my own signature, but seeking Muhammad Ali's. It was a moment of power for this lesser Black Ali!

Tonight in Abuja I am once again empowered by the company that I am keeping. The company includes Muhammad Ali and other luminaries. I am deeply moved.

The value of the occasion also arises from those who have organized it and have extended the recognition. The African Communications Agency is one of Africa's vanguard institutions in this era of the Information Superhighway. And ECOWAS is the most ambitious experiment in regional integration ever attempted by African peoples anywhere in the world. These two sponsors of the Living Legends Awards Ceremony have added immensely to the importance of this occasion.

It is also very important that Africa recognizes and salutes those who have served it while we are still around. I have been privileged to have lived and served in several African countries, lectured in dozens and written and broadcast about the whole of Africa and its Diaspora

Of course, my motivation was to serve Africa and serve the world of scholarship, rather than to seek recognition and awards. But when such recognition does come from my peers or my African compatriots or my colleagues in the academy and in the wider world of scholarship, it is always a humbling experience, deeply gratifying.

It was in 1957 that I entered the University of Manchester in England to start studying for my bachelor's degree. This year 2007 is the 50th anniversary of that start of my academic education as an undergraduate.

You are, therefore, honouring me on my Golden Jubilee from the year when I first entered a university as a student. 1957 was also the year when my future Nigerian wife was born. I was entering a university; Pauline was entering the world! On the wider stage of history was independent Ghana. Ghana also entered the world stage in 1957.

2007 is, therefore, a fitting celebration! I am very grateful to ECOWAS, to the African Communications Agency and to this International Media Summit of our beloved continent for honouring me in this manner.

God bless Africa and God bless us all. Amen.

Professor Ali Mazrui needs no introduction to any student of African politics. Recently nominated as one of the 100 greatest living public intellectuals in the world by the Washington-based journal, Foreign Policy, Professor Mazrui is the author of more than twenty books and hundreds of articles published all over the world. He was the author and narrator of the highly regarded television series The Africans: A Triple Heritage (BBC/PBS, 1986). He is currently Director of the Institute of Global Cultural Studies and Albert Schweitzer Professor in the Humanities, State University of New York at Binghamton. He is also Andrew D. White Professor-at-Large Emeritus and Senior Scholar in Africana Studies, Cornell University, Ithaca, New York, USA; Chancellor, Jomo Kenyatta University of Agriculture and Technology, Thika, Kenya as well as the Albert Luthuli Professor-at-Large at the University of Jos, Nigeria.

African Performance Review

APR

Annual Subscription Rates

Companies/orgs./institutions: £180
(including access to the online editions)

Individuals: online and Print: £60
Individuals: Online only: £30

Retail sales:
Individuals (print)   £20 (+ P&P)
Online   £10 per issue

To contribute, contact the journal's editor;

The Editor, (Dr Osita Okagbue)
Department of Drama, Goldsmiths, University of London,
SE14 6NW United Kingdom. Tel: +44 (0)207 919-7581.
Email: AfTA@gold.ac.uk.

Subscription enquiries,
please contact: sales@adonis-abbey.com

Adonis & Abbey Publishers Ltd
P.O. Box 43418,
London
SE11 4XZ
United Kingdom
Tel.: +44 (0) 2077938893

Book Review

African Renaissance
Vol. 4 No.1 Quarter 1 2007
pp118-121

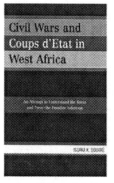

Civil Wars and Coup d'Etat in West Africa: An Attempt to Understand the Roots and Prescribe Solutions. Lanham: University Press of America Inc., pp.255. ISBN-10: 0-7618-3425-7; ISBN-13: 978-0-7618-3425-0
Author: Issaka K. Souare
Reviewer: Kenneth Omeje

Since post-colonial history, especially, during the past two decades, West Africa has earned notoriety as one of the world's most turbulent and poorest regions. Prebendal corruption, bad governance, military coup d'etat, warlord insurgency, state failure, civil war, lawlessness, and a myriad of low intensity communal conflicts have been some of the defining characteristics of some of the world's poorest countries of West Africa in recent decades. *Civil Wars and Coup d'Etat in West Africa* by Issaka K. Souare provides a rigorous and comprehensive analysis of the problem and consequences of political instability in West Africa. The author presents a systematic historical analysis of the problematic, exploring the nexus of causal and aggravating factors, as well as how they all play out in both the local and wider regional contexts. He further critiques the seemingly dominant orthodox western-centric perspective to [West] African civil wars and political instability, which tends to privilege notions of unbridled primordialism. Some of the Western-centric explanations, particularly the journalistic accounts of Western media and Afro-pessimists, tend to castigate African conflicts as irrational tendencies that bother on tribal, clannish, religious and historical animosities between irreconcilable primordial groups – tendencies that are believed to have a marked pejorative and primitivity slant. Closely related to this primordial explanation, or arguably misconception, is the tendency to virtually regard every persistent low intensity conflict in Africa, which is in most cases restricted to one section of a country, as civil war. Souare debunked this as hyperbole, arguing that such low intensity conflicts horridly branded civil wars in Africa can be likened to the violent conflicts in the British region of Northern Ireland, the French Brittany (Bretagne) and Corsica (Corse) and the Spanish Basque region.

While acknowledging the symptomatic and consequential effects of primordial factors like ethnicity and religion in West African civil wars and coups d'etat, the author argues that these factors are essentially secondary. He divided the instigating and aggravating factors of civil conflicts in West Africa into internal and external factors (p.8). With regard to the internal factors, Souare in chapters one and two located the causality on the political economy of neo-patrimonialism with its implications for bad governance, corruption, nepotism, cronyism, clientelism, flagrant abuse of legal and institutional order, as well as systematic exclusion, impoverishment and repression of the subalterns and disaffected groups. It is this pattern and cycle of neo-patrimonial misgovernance, the author argued, that more or less precipitated the recent civil wars in Liberia, Sierra Leone, Mali, Cote d'Ivoire and, to a lesser extent, the Biafra secessionist war in Nigeria (1967-1970). Most of the incidents of military coups d'etat, insurgency and counter-hegemonism in different West African countries also have a similar trend.

Concerning the external factors, Souare underscores and analyses in chapters two and three the nexus of vested international corporatist and neo-colonial interests in West Africa, leading to foreign political, diplomatic and military interventions by ex-colonial powers, especially France, to protect their "national" interests; the illicit trade in small arms and light weapons and the often jaundiced and inflammatory news reports of sections of the foreign media. The horrendous role of some powerful Western mining companies and arms dealers who often exploit political instability and wars in Africa to maximize unaccountable and illicit accumulation was particularly underscored as partly contributing to the prolongation of many civil conflicts and the apparent reluctance of the international community to initiate prompt and robust conflict prevention/peacekeeping intervention.

In chapter four, Souare details the devastating consequences of civil wars and coups d'etat in West Africa. Notable among them are grave internal consequences such as collapse of state governing institutions, including institutions of law and order; a culture of violence and impunity, humanitarian crisis and forced population displacement, collapse of formal/ informal [subsistent] economies and growth in underground or shadow economy, massive emigration of highly skilled manpower otherwise called brain-drain, societal fragmentation and proliferation of child combatants. Across the fragile international borders and at the wider (sub)regional level are problems of large-scale movement of refugees and combatants, including mercenaries; proliferation of illicit trade in small arms, drugs and 'conflict goods', especially lootable natural resources;

deplorable humanitarian tragedy, and occasional acrimony and subversion of war-affected states by unfriendly neighbouring states.

In chapters five, Souare explores functional remedies for solving the problem of civil wars and political instability in West Africa while in chapter six (the last chapter), he appraises the unique position of Nigeria as a regional hegemon and the implications of this for conflict management and security in West Africa. The author identified internal and external remedial measures for West African conflicts, which partly correspond to the observed nature and dimensions of the conflicts. Given that African countries have little control over most of the external conflict-instigating and aggravating factors such as the neo-colonial / corporate interests of certain imperial powers and global corporations, Souare argued that African countries should pay greater attention to addressing the internal factors of their conflicts where they comparatively have extensive control. He proposes the need to establish transparent and accountable democracies in the region, which he considers a necessary condition for economic development, qualitative improvement in the educational system and good governance. Genuine democracies will also help to reduce the tendency to resort to armed violence as a means of dispute settlement and to suffocate or positively undermine the business of international arms dealers that have vested interest in the perpetuation of wars and armed conflicts in West Africa.

With regard to the external remedies, Souare makes a multi-faceted proposal that involves non-violent conflict prevention through conflict early warning and multi-tract diplomacy; as well as conflict resolution and settlement based on appropriate peacekeeping and peacebuilding measures. These proposals are constructively crafted within the programmatic framework of inter-governmental security organisations such as the United Nations (UN), African Union (AU) and Economic Community of West African States (ECOWAS). He critically evaluates the recent mediative and peacekeeping efforts of both the UN and ECOWAS in a range of conflicts in the West African region (Sierra Leone, Liberia, Guinea Bissau, Cote d'Ivoire, Mali and Togo). He underscores the apparent reluctance and delay of the international community (UN inclusive) to deploy peacekeepers with appropriate mandate to West African wars - a situation contrasted by the proactive strides of ECOWAS in conflict prevention and resolution amidst the regional body's debilitating resource and logistical constraints.

Finally, the author endorses Nigeria's hegemonic role in West Africa as having been largely positive, not least from the standpoint of regional stability and security. He dismisses as unfounded and malicious the fears often expressed by many West African governments, especially those of the Francophone bloc that tend to portray Nigeria's hegemonic role as a sub-imperialist threat. This deep-seated phobia against Nigeria's hegemonic status, the author argues, has been chiefly orchestrated by some Western imperial powers, in particular France, to keep West African countries antagonistically divided on artificial linguistic lines for the ultimate benefit of the metropolitan West.

It suffices to say that the greatest contribution of Souare's book lies in the author's conceptual conflation of the problematics of civil wars and coups d'etat in West Africa, further demonstrating through rigorous analysis the complex interface of the underlying causal and aggravating variables. The book is well-researched and full of vital and credible information. The author's multi-lingual background proves a strategic advantage as empirical materials and literature used in the analysis of the book were of varied linguistic sources – English, French, and to a lesser extent, Arabic. Above all, the book is written in lucid and elegant prose, devoid of highfalutin technical jargons and phraseologies. This makes it reader-friendly and potentially amenable to a wide variety of audience. Even though a reader may not agree entirely with all the arguments in the book, especially the author's views on the controversial issues of primary causality of African civil conflicts, the place of primordialism in the structure of causalities and catalysts, the now-fashionable notion of "African solutions to Africa's problems", etc, there is no doubt that Souare has produced a timely and brilliant handbook on the subject of political instability in Africa. He has also articulated some serious thoughts on how to tackle the imbroglio. This book is a must read for everyone interested in understanding the nexus between political violence, instability and development or lack of it in Africa.

Kenneth Omeje
Africa Centre, Department of Peace Studies,
University of Bradford

Printed in the United Kingdom
by Lightning Source UK Ltd.
122362UK00001B/289-297/A